D1596201

The
Ego at the
Center
of Clinical
Technique

Critical Issues in ———
PSYCHOANALYSIS

clp₁

Editors:

Steven J. Ellman, Ph.D.
Arnold Wilson, Ph.D.

Editorial Board:

Corresponding Editor:

Michael Moskowitz, Ph.D.

The
Ego at the
Center
of Clinical
Technique

Fred Busch

JASON ARONSON INC.
Northvale, New Jersey
London

Production Editor: Judith D. Cohen

This book was set in 10 point Bookman by TechType of Upper Saddle River, New Jersey, and printed and bound by Haddon Craftsmen of Scranton, Pennsylvania.

Library of Congress Cataloging-in-Publication Data

Busch, Fred, 1939–
    The ego at the center of clinical technique / by Fred
Busch.
        p. cm.
    Includes bibliographical references and index.
        ISBN 1-56821-471-5
    1. Ego (Psychology) 2. Psychoanalysis. 3. Psychoanalytic
interpretation. 4. Ego strength. 5. Self-perception.
6. Personality change. I. Title.
    RC489.E35B87 1995
    616.89'17—dc20   94-46740

Manufactured in the United States of America. Jason Aronson Inc. offers books and cassettes. For information and catalog write to Jason Aronson Inc., 230 Livingston Street, Northvale, New Jersey 07647.

To Barbara, Chris, and Joshua

CONTENTS

Part II
The Ego in Contemporary Clinical Thought

FOREWORD: ACHIEVING LASTING STRUCTURAL CHANGE

In this insightful work, Fred Busch undertakes further elaboration of contemporary structural theory and refines new ways of looking at and understanding its technical implications for clinical psychoanalysis. Written with a clear and engaging pen, this book is accessible to both students and practitioners of psychotherapy and psychoanalysis. This erudite volume is destined to take its place next to Fenichel's, Glover's, Greenson's, and Gray's volumes as one of the classics in psychoanalytic technique. It is rare to find such a smooth and well-articulated integration of theory and practice as evidenced by the small number of books with which Dr. Busch's can be readily compared.

This book is important. Its clear and concise thoughts about the analytic process combined with its theoretical and clinical sophistication demonstrates the vitality and creativity of contemporary psychoanalysis. It is a remarkably modern work, not at all a rehashing of old ideas or a blanket endorsement of what is already known. Dr. Busch offers a

refreshing and timely contribution to the furthering of
modern-day Freudian thought. He again and again demonstrates that close, careful attention to the technical implications of Freud's structural model leads to profound
alterations away from the older model of the analyst as a
distant authority figure, toward a newer model of the collaborative analytic endeavor. The contemporary analyst, in Fred
Busch's view, moves inevitably toward greater sensitivity in
addressing the conscious ego. He approvingly cites Gray's
(1982) aphorism that "the therapeutic results of analytic
treatment are lasting in proportion to the extent to which
during the analysis the patient's unbypassed ego functions
have become involved in a consciously and increasingly
voluntary co-partnership with the analyst" (p. 264). It is Dr.
Busch's mission to explicate exactly how this unique benefit
of psychoanalytic work, *lasting structural change,* can take
place.

His work—as well as that of the colleagues whom he
cites—illustrates that there *is* a contemporary structural
approach to psychoanalysis, one grounded in the theory of
ego psychology. It is important to reiterate this point, since it
is often wrongly thought that classical analysis is a field that
resists modernization. Many analysts in the last decade have
turned their attentions toward the pursuit of overcoming
what Gray has pointed to as a "developmental lag" in
psychoanalysis. Overcoming this lag involves a repudiation
of many of the clinical assumptions that follow from the use
of Freud's topographic model, in particular its technical
emphasis on making the unconscious conscious through
interpretation. In retrospect, it is now clear that theoretical
exploration of the tripartite model of the mind introduced by
Freud in 1923 and elaborated in 1926 far outpaced the study
and understanding of its technical implications.

Central to Busch's work is a respectful sensitivity to the
importance of the ego and the role it plays in giving rise to the
symptoms and/or character traits for which our patients seek
help. Dr. Busch's approach to analytic technique can seem
deceptively simple because of its solid grounding in his

understanding of pathogenesis. He approaches his patients with the view that their symptoms, defenses, and resistances derive from intrapsychic conflict. It is his conviction that all psychological problems, or, for that matter, all analytic behavior, involves compromise formations among different mental strutures. This guides his technical strategies. Mindful that anxiety and other threatening affects fuel compromise formations and promote the layering of defense and content, he is careful to analyze from the surface downward. At the same time, he always keeps in mind the fundamental assumption that bypassing the ego will likely increase the patient's anxiety. This at worst undermines the analytic work, and at best leads to a passive submission to the analyst. When this happens, symptom resolution and/or characterological change based on such identifications with the analyst are doomed to be fragile because of the failure to develop the self-analyzing ability that Dr. Busch's close monitoring approach promotes. The identification is then with the analyst, not the analyst's purpose. Without the presence of the analyst, work cannot proceed.

The close monitoring approach to analyzing the ego that Dr. Busch describes thoughout the book allows for an analytic focus on those aspects of ego functioning that perpetuate conflicts and thus serve to restrict thinking. In this light, analytic goals are usefully conceptualized in terms of greater freedom of thought and the capacity for self-analysis. Technically, Dr. Busch depicts methods remarkable for their consistent focus on such goals. Thus, interpretations must be formulated in ways that will be "in the neighborhood," that is, accessible to the patient's ego. Over and over again, the reader is reminded that what the patient can hear and work with is more important than what the analyst knows and can formulate. In fascinating detail, Fred Busch demonstrates how begining the analysis and teaching the fundamental rule take on great importance because of the goal of making the analytic process understandable to the patient, rather than fostering the artificial creation of the image of an omniscient analyst who then runs the risk of being seen as acting upon a passive, receptive analysand. Developing an analytic relationship that sees actions of all sorts as communications with subtle yet profound implications for developing higher levels of ego functioning is carefully explicated.

Resistance analysis is a central component of Dr. Busch's approach, so that the patient's resistance to optimally using the analytic process becomes a major focus of intervention. It is in this way that the goal of self-analysis is best realized. It is in this context that Dr. Busch describes analytic listening—monitoring the ongoing flow of processes for subtle disruptions, gaps in associations, or other shifts in form or content of associations, in order to ferret out the hidden and seemingly slight resistances. When further analyzed, such small details will often be shown to be connected to an unconscious fantasy that is prescribing types of action. Thus, the form of an association is usually as or more important than the content. How forms of thought are made manifest through the entire repertoire of communicative skills can shed light on fluctuations in the ego indicative of resistance.

Dr. Busch fills his book with beautiful, detailed clinical vignettes in order to demonstrate his views in a way that is accessible to the reader. He thus illustrates his points, and allows readers to park themselves next to him, looking over his shoulder at a master clinician at work. What these vignettes demonstrate is that he is anything but the caricature of the silent, aloof classical analyst. He is quite active in pursuing and exploring shifts in associations. Likewise, this approach is so clearly based in the here and now, the flow of ongoing processes, that one wonders whether he advocates a historical focus at all. However, Dr. Busch makes it clear he does not eschew other components of what has been central to the task of analysis over the years. He believes, though, that a focus on the role of the ego in psychoanalysis has remained underdeveloped. Thus, there is a need for a book like this one that highlights this component of the analytic task. The sensitivity and skill that he shows in detecting subtle hints of resistance in the analytic present, his emphasis on involving the patient as an active co-partner in the analytic enterprise whose goal is to be able to eventually anlayze himself without the aid of the analyst, as well as his requirement that interventions be formulated in words that the patient can hear and integrate, render it now clear that psychoanalysis has a model that is quite different from the common caricature.

As with any new inquiry into therapeutic technique, questions inevitably emerge. For example, whether more disturbed patients may, at times, require some immediate affective connection with the therapist than closely following the process may offer, or whether Dr. Busch's formulations are applicable to work with children, are two issues that stand to benefit from further investigation. Only clinical reports by analysts who embark upon such experiments will allow us to answer such questions.

While passionate in his defense of the central role of the ego to the analytic enterprise, Dr. Busch sees his model of treatment as a highly useful technique to be used with greater or lesser frequency in the analysis of any patient. The question as to how and when to mobilize this approach becomes a diagnostic one, depending upon any person's ability to make use of it at any particular time. Thus, one can imagine working in this way so as to promote a self-analytic capacity, being sure not to bypass the ego functions necessary for a fully cooperative analytic undertaking, and yet utilize other aspects of technique as well.

Dr. Busch has made a profound contribution to contemporary structural psychoanalysis. In elaborating such a clear and well-delineated technical strategy, he has raised a vision of psychoanalysis into a view that has far-reaching reverberations. Now, it is up to practicing analysts to see how such an approach fares with their analysands. We are all joined in the common interest of furthering the evolution of modern psychoanalytic thought, to which this book makes a momentous contribution.

Arnold Wilson, Ph.D. and Alan Sugarman, Ph.D.
New York City and San Diego
March, 1995

ACKNOWLEDGMENTS

I was at a meeting of the International Psychoanalytic Association when a speaker got up and voiced many of the concerns and questions I had been raising. These revolved around my impression that in clinical presentations and the discussions that followed, technical considerations seemed dominated by Freud's Topographic Model. I went up to the speaker after the meeting, and we spoke only long enough for me to learn his name—Cecilio Paniagua, a Baltimore-Washington-trained psychoanalyst who had since moved back to his native country, Spain. We also talked briefly of our mutual interests. He suggested I might want to read the work of Paul Gray and, furthermore, that he might be interested in seeing my work.

Never has a piece of advice had such a profound effect on my thinking. I started poring over Gray's papers, which resulted in a flood of thoughts about the analytic process. It has been my impression that most therapists who seriously study his work are similarly affected, but a surprising number consign it to the category of "we always did that." Yet it is clear in listening to their clinical examples that they do not do "that." In my own work I have begun to look at the ego in a somewhat different context, yet Paul Gray's work remains as a stimulus for most of what I have written. I believe his work will stand as a major creative contribution to psycho-analytic thinking.

Personally, I have been appreciative of the generosity of Gray's interest in my work. When not in agreement with me, Gray has been a formidable intellectual antagonist, but al-ways within a spirit of inquiry, respect, and goodwill. I would also include Anton Kris's book and papers on the method of free association as another series of work that has had a profound effect on how I understand the analytic process.

No one reaches the stage of at least thinking he has enough to say to write a book without a lot of encouragement and stimulation. I feel fortunate in this regard, but limitations in space prohibit me from acknowledging all those who have been so helpful. Thus, I will present only a partial list. First, I would like to thank my mentors, and now colleagues, at the Michigan Psychoanalytic Institute, who with courage and foresight offered psychoanalytic training to a number of psy-chologists when this was far from the norm in institutes of the American Psychoanalytic Association. Marvin Margolis, who has been so influential in American psychoanalysis, with an occasional encouraging word or challenging question was central in my involvement with first our own institute, then the American Psychoanalytic Association. It was serendipi-tous to have had contact with numerous psychologists throughout my early training who had, or were in the midst of analytic training. When I was a psychology intern at the University of Colorado Medical Center in the early '60s, there were two psychologists, Dick Waite and the late Mark Rud-nick, who were flying to Chicago along with other candidates from Denver for analytic training. As a postdoctoral fellow at the Reiss-Davis Child Study Center, I met a number of psy-chologists who had been trained in child analysis at the Hamp-stead Clinic, along with Rudi Ekstein, who was trained as a psychoanalyst in Europe. It left me with a belief that psychoanalytic training was more possible than reality at the time would have dictated.

Teachers who helped me understand the value of the ego in clinical psychoanalysis, in order of occurrence, were: Joe Dodds and Bob Martin, my psychological testing supervisors during an internship at the University of Colorado Medical Center, who were the first to help me learn about the role of the ego, without labeling it as such; Chris Heinike, who directed a nursery school observational research project at the Reiss-Davis Child Study Center that furthered my understanding of adaptation in psychological functioning and fostered an appreciation for careful observation as a useful source of psychological information; at the University of Michigan Medical Center, Humberto Nagera, who developed an extraordinary preschool program for research and training that furthered my understanding of the developmental phases of the ego; and at the Michigan Psychoanalytic Institute, Mayer Subrin, who helped me understand the value of staying closely tied to the clinical material. In my analyses I learned about the power of unconscious fantasies within an atmosphere of respect for the significance of the ego.

Many colleagues have read early drafts of my work and offered helpful comments. Kerry and Jack Novick were especially encouraging as I began to work out my ideas, Cecilio Paniagua has remained a supportive and helpful critic, while Barry Landau's comments and questions always cause me to clarify my thinking. A particular candidate class at the Michigan Psychoanalytic Institute (Glenn Good, James Hansell, Robert LaCoste, Bill Nixon, Michael Singer, Susan Wainright, and Mark Ziegler), by their questions and interest, challenged me to expand my thinking in a very beneficial manner. As graduate students in psychology at the University of Michigan, now both Ph.D.'s, Kimberlyn Leary and Jennifer Stuart were receptive and inquisitive in a stimulating way . Finally, in many discussions with my friend and now academic associate at the Michigan Psychoanalytic Institute, Professor Howard Kamler, I was forced to define my ideas in a coherent, jargon-free way that furthered my thinking.

PART I

ISSUES OF
TECHNIQUE

1

THINKING IN
A NEW WAY

The thesis of this book is that we must place more emphasis on the role of the ego in our understanding and interventions in the therapeutic setting. In many ways we are still wedded to Freud's topographic model, with its primary emphasis on bringing what is unconscious into consciousness. While not eschewing the power of the unconscious to affect mental life, the topographic model reflects an erroneous theory of how the mind works, with only a rudimentary appreciation for what were later called ego functions. As a basis for the change process in psychoanalysis, the topographic model leads to certain technical errors. Thus, what is bypassed with the topographic model as a clinical exemplar are the detailed ways by which the ego defends against awareness of, while simultaneously gratifying, unconscious fantasies; how defenses undertaken early in life as a means of adaptation to a frightening situation affect both the means by which the past is represented in the present, and the method and timing of analytic interventions; and the method by which structural changes occur in the ego that are a necessary part of an analytic cure.

It is impressive how many of the newer theories in psychoanalysis are based, in part, on a rejection of Freud's earliest model of the mind and its application to the analytic process. In these theories it is as if the structural model was never introduced. A good example can be found in the work of Malin (1993). In trumpeting the value of the self-psychological view of resistances in contrast to what he considers the traditional perspective, Malin states that the self-psychological view recognizes how "the 'resistances' represent the best, indeed the only, adaptive means of self protection available to the patient at a given time" (p. 506). Yet Freud's (1926) second theory of anxiety clearly suggests such a position, and this perspective has been explicated by a number of therapists (Apfelbaum and Gill 1989, Busch 1992, Gray 1973, 1982, 1986, 1990a,b, 1992, Schafer 1983, Stone 1973).

I would submit that such confusion is based on wide-spread misunderstanding of an ego-psychological approach, due to a long-standing lag in articulating the usefulness of an ego-analytic method for clinical psychoanalysis. While there are certain shibboleths associated with ego psychology born out of the structural model—that is, interpret defense before content, and work with the ego before the id—the manner in which these are to be operationalized has not been sufficiently elaborated in a way that has been helpful to many therapists. Meanwhile, the variety of ways the ego needs to be considered in order for effective analysis to occur remains at the level of clinical lore, inadequately passed on, if at all. The irony is that many of these newer theories seem to be describing disturbances in *ego* states that affect not only the thematic content of hours but the techniques by which the therapist may best be useful to the patient (Busch 1995b).

EGO CHANGES IN PSYCHOANALYSIS

There is a shift we expect as a *sine qua non* of a successful analysis that exemplifies the enormous significance of the modification of the ego to the change process in psychoanalysis. This shift is captured in the following sequence. After a period of analytic work has been done with the patient's resistances to experiencing the transference, it is common for a patient to be convinced that, based on the way the therapist opened the waiting room door, or smiled, or did not smile, or said, "hello," that the therapist is in a particular mood. If asked to reflect on this perception when it first occurs, the patient is often confused, believing such a question is like being asked to wonder about the observation that a 6'10" male is tall. The patient is convinced, if he thinks the therapist looked angry about something, it is only because the therapist looked angry. At a later time in the analysis, this same patient, having the same perception of the therapist, would likely have developed a striking new capacity. This new capacity, which is nothing less than a change in the ability to think about events, leads the patient to at least wonder why it is he noticed that aspect of the therapist's demeanor even if his perception was correct. In short, the patient now has the capacity to observe his or her own observations—a crucial component of a self-analytic process. It is an example of a specific structural change in the ego that Loewald (1971) described more broadly when he depicted the curative process in psychoanalysis as dependent upon experiences previously unavailable to higher-level ego functions now being available, which thus opens "up the possibility of the ego's organizing activity exerting itself" (p. 62).

The higher-level ego functions that develop in analysis are manifested in changes in the way a patient can think about him- or herself, and about thoughts. Thus, the type of thinking characteristic of the patient early in treatment is typical for that period of time when the infantile neurosis first develops. In this manner of thinking, described first in the child development literature by Piaget (1926), the child feels no need to justify his reasoning to others. Neither does he search for contradictions in his logic. He cannot reconstruct a chain of reasoning through which he has just passed. One can say he thinks but he cannot think about his thinking.

Thinking during this development period, as in the beginning patient, takes on a type of "phenomenal, before-the-eye reality" (Flavell 1963, p. 203). In the patient's mind it is something akin to believing "if it seems that way to me it must be true." It is many years before a type of thinking develops that mirrors the patient's thinking at a later stage in analysis. Again, this developmental stage in thinking is captured by Flavell (1963) when he states:

> No longer exclusively preoccupied with the sober business of trying to stabilize and organize just what comes directly to the senses, the adolescent has, through this new orientation, the potentiality of imagining all that might be there—both the very obvious and the very subtle—and thereby better insuring the finding of all that is there. [p. 205]

This is the type of thinking that allows the patient to observe his observations. It is not tied to the concrete realities of thoughts but has the flexibility to imagine such things as whatever the patient thinks about the therapist may be a manifestation of his own thought process. It is a crucial development in the capacity for self-analysis that I would consider the hallmark of a successful analysis. As seen in the work of Schlesinger and Robbins (1983), successful analyses are characterized by a capacity to use the self-analytic process in response to revived conflicts.

What I am pointing to, then, is that specific changes occur in the ego during successful analyses. *It is not the core unconscious fantasies of the patient that change. These remain intact, ready to be stimulated. What does change is the patient's capacity to think about his or her conflicts.* This ability is captured in the patient's greater freedom to know what he is thinking and, just as importantly, the patient's capacity to think about his or her thinking. This latter point has not been sufficiently emphasized in the psychoanalytic literature. It represents an approach to analysis that is indifferent to the necessity of the patient's participation in the process beyond saying what comes to mind.

The changes in thought process I am describing are crucial in replacing the *inevitability of action by the possibility of thought*. The patient who always finds himself involved with sadistic women, for example, develops the capacity in a successful analysis to observe the implications of his be-havior and then make a choice. He did not have this choice before.

ANALYTIC TECHNIQUE

Certain principles follow from the perspective that the pri-mary changes that take place in analysis are in the ego. Broadly these principles suggest that (1) the focus of the analysis now revolves around those aspects of ego func-tioning that keep conflicts alive and restrict thinking, and (2) analytic goals are more fruitfully conceived of in terms of greater freedom of thought and the capacity for self-analysis. At the same time, the therapist's technique may, in a variety of ways, facilitate progressive or regressive forces in the ego. In general, this can be seen in the degree to which the therapist's stance is more authoritarian, in contrast to an approach that seeks to include the patient as a coparticipant. In specific ways, the therapist's attempts to include the ego in the process can be seen in such things as how much attention the therapist pays to what the *patient* can hear rather than what the *therapist* knows (see Chapter 2); how much the therapist makes the *process* understandable to the patient (see Chapter 3); how much the patient's resistances to using the process are analyzed (see Chapter 5); how much we attempt to make the basis of our interpretations understand-able to the patient (see Chapter 4); and how much the therapist takes into account such things as the *form* in which the material appears (see Chapter 6).

Analyzing the ego as the center of one's orientation to the analytic hour lends a different cast to the analytic work, as illustrated in the following case. A middle-aged woman came into her analytic session with the observation that she was upset with her husband over the weekend, and it puzzled her. She could see that he was being a pain, but it was the extent of her upset that she wondered about. She got mad at him on Saturday and wanted nothing to do with him the rest of the day. Earlier in the week they had agreed to do yard work on Saturday. There was no other place in their schedule to do it for the next few weeks, and the yard was starting to look seedy. That morning her husband had been invited to play golf. He declined the invitation but complained the whole time about what he gave up. In angry tones she talked about how infantile he could be. After angrily describing various examples of this behavior, she paused briefly, then went on to describe how he is really a pretty good guy, especially in comparison to what she hears from her friends about their husbands. I noted she had been talking in an angry tone about her husband, there was a brief pause, and then her whole demeanor in relation to describing him changed. I wondered whether she could remember anything from the pause that might have led her to move away from her angry feelings. Now that I brought her attention to it, she said, she had a fleeting image of her mother with a particular house-coat on. This reminded her of the family ritual of cleaning the house every Saturday morning. It didn't matter what else was occurring—everybody had to be up early to pitch in and help. She remembered numerous sleepovers she was invited to that she couldn't attend, because her mother was convinced it would interfere with her full participation the following day. She never said anything to her mother, as she was fearful of her mother's rage. I suggested that from what she had said, it seemed understandable why she became upset. Here it is, another "must" cleaning situation, and her husband felt free to express *his* dissatisfaction. In her mind, to do so is associated with being in a dangerous situation, like facing her mother's attacks. The danger she still felt when angry feelings arose could be seen in her sudden need to undo these feelings, when the image of her mother came to mind. Thus, her husband's freedom to express his discontent, and her feelings of anger with him, both felt dangerous to her. As she saw her husband, rather than her own feelings as the cause of this danger, it is understandable she would feel upset with him.

After hearing this vignette, many analysts would immediately start to speculate as to underlying fantasies behind the patient's upset and anger—the "deep divers," as one colleague described them. Thus, they might begin to wonder whether the patient's associations to a sleepover were a reference to a wish to sleep with the therapist over the weekend, and whether her angry response to her husband's complaints was based on her guilty feelings over this wish. I would not consider these notions incorrect, just premature. What I was first struck by is the patient's observations. She could feel and be aware of her upset over the weekend, without needing to undo it before the analytic hour. Furthermore, she could report a sense that there was something in the intensity of her feelings that did not quite fit the situation. Thus, we see the patient able to engage in a self-observational process. She has also been able to observe angry feelings that, as we see in the hour, are still dangerous for her. While doing this, she can allow herself to have the uncomfortable sense there is something amiss in the intensity of her reaction to the anger. This is the point where the ego seems to have gotten in the work. At the same time, we can see the ego's defensive activity. This is the perfect time to work with a resistance, as it is occurring in a readily observable form for both the patient and therapist. No conjecture need be made about some hypothetical defensive state, as the resistance process is there in concrete form.

This concreteness is an important component of the interpretive process, in that the patient's thinking is most concrete in areas of conflict (see Chapters 4 and 6). At the same time, I am trying, in my interpretation, to utilize in thought and word the patient's own associations. In this manner, I try to stay with what the patient is most conscious of (i.e., his words), without straining the patient's credulity. Thus, in my interpretation to the patient, I use what she has already been able to observe or what we have observed in the session (e.g., the sudden change in tone). I treat the patient's associations as the data of analysis, and interventions should flow from these associations in a way that is understandable to the patient. In this manner, I try to de-mystify the interpretive process, making it less dependent on special powers or knowledge of the therapist (see Chapter 2). I invite the patient to use certain ego functions in evaluating the data with me. This, I believe, is a crucial part in the development of an analytic stance that highlights self-analysis A passive ego is antithetical to such a stance. Thus, the patient's ego is at the forefront of my work, in considering both the optimal working surface and how to use the data of analysis.

Another useful conceptualization of my therapeutic intervention is in the language of ego syntonicity/dystonicity. In everyday parlance this perspective captures a central concept in ego analysis—that is, interpreting at a level that is comfortable enough for the patient so she doesn't have to reject the interpretation, while not being so comfortable that it is irrelevant to the process of resolving conflict. Landau (in press) recently called this concept (i.e., ego syntonicity/ dystonicity) "appealing," in that it was close to the structural model and "would also highlight the idea of the ego as an organization, which integrates syntonic elements, but which in its defensive mode, dissociates elements that are dystonic."

Apfelbaum and Gill (1989) have also commented on the significance of this conceptualization for an ego-analytic approach, especially in gauging what is acceptable to interpret in the wish–defense oscillation. From this view, the patient described earlier came in with an observation about herself that was in the space between syntonicity/dystonicity (i.e., being bothered by how upset she became when angry with her husband). However, even though she was upset over her anger, she was able to keep it in mind and talk about it in spite of her discomfort. The anger she experienced in the session was more dystonic, apparently because an association came to mind about this having to do with her mother and the danger associated with that. However, my question in the exploration of her defense allowed her to bring the dangerous connection back into her mind. Therefore, it now seemed less dystonic. My interpretation, then, was of what was uncomfortable but tolerable. The upset, the anger, and the association with her mother all were uncomfortable, but not so much that they needed to remain alien to her ego. I attempted to speak to issues that were within tolerable levels of discomfort, thus leading her not to have to reject her thoughts. This whole issue of ego syntonicity/dystonicity seems a promising line of thinking about the clinical enterprise while highlighting an ego-analytic approach.[1]

THE LAG IN EGO ANALYSIS

Until Gray's (1982) classic "developmental lag" paper, it was not well understood that there had been little in the way of any systematic attempt to understand the significance of the ego in clinical technique. Freud (1923) considered his discussion of the structural theory only the "roughest outline" (p. 12), and all his major clinical papers appeared long before the introduction of this model. Gray (1982) and I (Busch1992) have shown that even after his introduction of the structural model, Freud frequently reverted back to topographic ways of thinking when discussing clinical situations. Thus, Freud's major contributions to ego psychology (i.e., the ego as the seat of anxiety, unconscious ego resistances, and the recognition that unconscious fantasies were highly organized and structured) were integrated into clinical technique at the time in only a cursory fashion. Elaborations on clinical technique that used the new ego psychology were made by Reich (1933) and Sterba (1934), but the major contributions at the

---

1. Throughout these chapters I will be using descriptive psychoanalytic terms that express similar notions (e.g., the ability to become conscious of particular thoughts or feelings without too much discomfort), although I think what Landau (in press) called the "complex and difficult undertaking" of learning to apply the concepts ego syntonicity/dystonicity to the clinical setting would be a fruitful step for ego analysis.

time were produced by Anna Freud (1936), in *The Ego and Mechanisms of Defense*, and in a little-known paper by Searl (1936; see Chapter 8). Pray (1994) demonstrates how A. Freud's method of resistance analysis, a forerunner of Gray's work, "essentially disappeared from the literature, including Anna Freud's own writings" (p. 88). The same is true of Searl's work. A. Freud heralded this possibility when presenting her then-new method of defense analysis.

> There have been periods in the development of psychoanalytical science when the theoretical study of the individual ego was distinctly unpopular. Somehow or other, many analysts conceived the idea that, in analysis, the value of the scientific and therapeutic work done was in direct proportion to the *depth* of the psychic strata upon which attention was focused. Whenever interest was transferred from the deeper to the more superficial psychic strata—whenever, that is to say, research was deflected from the id to the ego—it was felt that here was a beginning apostasy from psychoanalysis as a whole. [1936, p. 3]

Eerie in its prescience is Ernst Kris's (1938) warning that the subtle but significant changes in technique trumpeted by Miss Freud "might pass unnoticed" (p. 347).

The "Golden Age" of psychoanalytic ego psychology has usually been associated with the work of Hartmann (1939, 1960, 1964), Hartmann and colleagues (1946, 1949), and Rapaport (1967). Yet, their works are barely referred to in the literature anymore, perhaps because of their emphasis on the development of psychoanalysis as a general psychology and their relative neglect of issues related to clinical technique. The enduring contributions of these authors have been to the understanding of the structure of the personality via the elaboration of the functioning of the ego as both an autonomous entity and a force vis à vis the id and superego and to the elaboration of the unfolding stages in ego development in interaction with environmental factors. This work set the stage for our comprehending, for example, the devastating effects of the psychological and/or physical absence of parental figures throughout childhood and adolescence, which became crucial in our understanding borderline and narcissistic disorders. Unfortunately, the works of these early ego psychologists were firmly rooted in Freud's ill-conceived energy theory leading to change still being seen as the result of cathexes redistribution, and it is possible to see those identified as structural theorists continuing to view differences in patients based on the "intensity" of conflict rather than qualities in ego functioning (Arlow 1985).

Gray (1973, 1982, 1986, 1990a,b, 1991, 1992, 1994) is the first analyst to consistently apply the principles of ego psychology to the technique of psychoanalysis in a systematic fashion. His work will be reviewed in a thoroughgoing manner throughout the book, so I will make no attempt to examine or critique it here. However, it is not widely understood that there are two major themes in Gray's ego psychology. One is the analysis of resistances, which is the part of his theory most therapists are familiar with. However, a second theme directly follows from his work with resistances, but it can be interpreted as a more general, philosophical approach to the ego throughout a psychoanalysis. More specifically, it is an approach that strongly suggests that we find ways to include the ego as a more active coparticipant in the analytic process, and sees the result of treatment dependent upon not bypassing key ego functions so that there is a consciously and increasingly voluntary co-partnership with the analyst. It is this line of thinking that I have elaborated in my own work.

SIGNIFICANCE OF THE EGO IN WORK WITH MORE DISTURBED PATIENTS

While the focus of these chapters is on interventions with neurotic range patients, they should also shed light on a number of important issues in working with more disturbed patients. I believe that in working analytically with borderline and

severely narcissistic patients, many therapists tend to neglect the importance of the ego. A general tendency seems to
be to bypass the ego for a direct interpretation of unconscious
thoughts or feelings, which lead potentially to even greater
regression than might be necessary in these individuals, with
a tendency to experience frequent regressions in ego functioning. It would seem that treating borderline and severly
narcissistic patients would require careful inclusion of the
ego. Yet tendencies to bypass the more mature components
of the patient's ego functions, which lead to a greater passivity and infantilization of the ego, seem to be more the rule
than the exception.

Let me start with a recent example from Steiner (1994).
The patient, having just recovered from what is described as
a "major breakdown" and being "very paranoid," was complaining about his employers and the therapist for not doing
enough for him. He then described a breast infection his
mother had when he was a baby and triumphantly spoke of
his ability to hurt the therapist. This was followed by an
announcement of his intention to take a new job, which
would necessitate a move to another city and the end of his
analysis.

> The analyst felt sad at the idea of losing his patient and
> interpreted that the patient wanted to get rid of his own
> sadness and wanted him, the analyst, to feel the pain of
> separation and loss. The patient said, "Yes, I can do to
> you what you do to me. You are in my hands. There is an
> equalization." A moment later he started to complain he
> was being poisoned and he began to discuss government
> policies of nuclear deterrence. . . . He then complained of
> gastric troubles and diarrhea and said he had been going
> to the toilet after each session recently. He explained that
> he had to shit out every word the analyst gave him in
> order not to be contaminated by infected milk. [p. 409]

Immediately striking is the therapist's conveyance of *a
way of thinking that is not that far, in form, from the*

patient's. In his interpretation, the therapist expresses the message "If I am feeling a particular way, it is because you have made me feel this way." The patient's almost immediate decompensation is followed by feelings of being poisoned, the difficulty in deterring nuclear attacks, and his need to "shit out" the therapist's remarks. Not only is there an ego regression going on in the patient, but his manner of thinking (i.e., the therapist's words are getting inside and poisoning him) mirrors in extreme how the therapist is thinking. The therapist's presentation of a particular way of thinking, without any modification or explanation, can only be frightening to such a patient who is prone to ego regression. It isn't that such processes, as the analyst describes, don't occur. It simply isn't usable information by the patient unless it is made understandable to the ego. The true art of analysis is finding a way to convey such complex feelings to a regressed patient in a manner the ego can grasp that isn't destructive. In addition to everything else in this example, the therapist is asking the patient's ego to take a passive, accepting role of the therapist's authority—a chancy process at best for an ego already prone to regression. It is an especially questionable technique in working with a paranoid patient, whose preoccupations with being invaded lead to an especially intense need to control others. The form in which the interpretation takes place disregards this and does not attempt to include the ego as part of the process.

Kernberg's (1987) method of working with more disturbed patients comes closer to what I will be describing in these chapters. His emphasis is on the use of the patient's free associations, and the exploration of unconscious meaning of behavior, to gain evidence before any hypothetical origin of behavior is explicated. An attempt is made, then, to use the data of analysis to bring into consciousness what is unfamiliar to the patient in a way that includes his or her thoughts as part of the process. It is a way of working that attempts to make the work of analyzing more understandable to the ego and determined less by what must be experienced by the patient as the therapist's magical or

idiosyncratic thought processes. This seems especially important in working with those patients whose own way of
thinking is subject to sudden regressive turns, dominated by
magical and idiosyncratic thought processes.

Another striking aspect of Steiner's interpretation, is
that he is *treating the patient's words as actions rather
than associations. Talking* about leaving the analysis is not
the same as *leaving* the analysis. The patient then reacts
similarly, treating the therapist's words as actions, albeit at a
more severe level (i.e., he is being poisoned and contami-
nated by the therapist's words, which leads him to need to
expel them). For patients who already have the tendency to
equate words with actions, the therapist who does the same
with little or no explanation will likely have a regressive
effect.

Being given the opportunity to discuss an elegant paper
on work with a borderline patient by Buie (1993) led me to
realize the importance of considering the ego in work with
these patients from another perspective. Buie reported that
for two years his patient refused to face him. Eventually the
patient explained that he was so full of rage with the therapist
that he feared his direct gaze would shatter the therapist's
head into slivers of glass. In this we see the patient taking an
action (i.e., facing away) as a means of dealing with a fantasy
that seems real to him. For two years the fantasy must be
undone by an action. The patient obviously felt the fantasy
could not be expressed or looked at as a "thought." For him
it was a frightening reality that could not even be said in
words. It is an excellent example of one factor in the borderline patients' world feeling so frightening to them and what
greatly complicates their ability to use a therapeutic process
(i.e., the borderlines' difficulty, at times, in distinguishing
between their thoughts as reality rather than a fantasy, and
certain compensatory beliefs in their own omnipotence; Novick and Novick 1991). Thus, Buie's patient treated the
fantasy that his gaze would shatter the therapist as a reality,
which led him to need to turn away.

My contention is that unless one closely analyzes the
ego's manner of organizing and responding to the inner and

outer world, idiosyncrasies in thinking will continue and thwart our analytic understanding and empathy. The patient's very sense of safety in the therapy will often depend on such analyses, which helps make understandable why a look, mood, or word frequently becomes a dangerous act for the borderline patient. It is just these kinds of difficulties in thinking that Buie's patient demonstrates in his inability to face the analyst for two years. The patient shows a way of thinking organized according to laws of perception and cognition that are either regressed or fixated, which continue to operate outside of consciousness. Any new information or experience will be responded to based upon the theories and structures of this way of thinking. What persists into adulthood, then, is not only the *content* of past memories but *structures* representing ways of thinking (e.g., conceptions of causality). Given the borderline's primitive thought processes and the sense of danger or destructiveness they present for them, attention must be paid to these ways of thinking in order for the patient to approach a sense of safety. Otherwise, these methods of thought will continue to flourish, contributing to the patient's sense of danger. Thus, one's therapeutic technique is altered depending on whether the borderline is seen as primarily suffering from primitive fantasies or disturbances in ego functioning. In the former, one would be looking to elaborate the primitive unconscious fantasy motivating the disturbed behavior; in the latter, one would be more focused on analyzing primitive ways of thinking. Of course, this does not have to be an either-or proposition. However, in the literature on working with more disturbed patients, it is clearly the emphasis on working with the patient's more disturbed ways of thinking based upon structured ways of looking at the world that has been most neglected.

CANT OR PERSPECTIVE

In discussions with colleagues on the slant of the following chapters, I have frequently been reminded of a joke. An elderly gentleman goes to his doctor, complaining of his wife's increasing deafness and her unwillingness to consider this a problem. He wonders whether there is a simple examination he can perform at home to prove to his wife how hard-of-hearing she has become. The doctor assures him there is, telling him that when he arrives home, he should yell something to his wife at five places of decreasing distance from her. The point at which she finally hears him will determine the degree of her disability. Armed with this information, the man returns home. From the front door he yells out, "Hi, honey, I'm home. What's for lunch?" There was no answer. He then went to the living room and yelled out the same thing, with similar results. With growing consternation he performs the experiment at two other places, and still no answer. Finally, in desperation, he comes up right behind her in the kitchen and yells again, "Hi, honey, I'm home. What's for lunch?" She then turns to him and says, with exasperation, "For the fifth time, chicken."

In these chapters I will be focusing primarily on one component of analytic interventions, the role of the ego. I will not attempt to cover all aspects of what comprises analytic understanding. Thus, the reader will frequently see some other element in the clinical material that he may have responded to, whether in the form of an unconscious wish, an aspect of the transference, an enactment, and so on. These chapters are not an attempt to negate the significance of a variety of ways of understanding the clinical interaction. Instead, they take one perspective and look at its effect on how we understand and approach a variety of aspects of the analytic situation. In a point to be elaborated on in Chapter 10, it is a familiar approach in scientific experiments to isolate a variable in order to see its effects upon other phenomena investigated. In this context, when a question is raised about some aspect of a clinical interaction being ignored, it can reflect a certain lack of understanding of the role of the ego and a way of approaching clinical phenomena. As in the joke, the question of who has not been hearing whom needs to be considered.

2

INTERPRETING "IN THE NEIGHBORHOOD"

The phrase "In the neighborhood" comes from Freud's (1910a) paper on "'Wild' Psycho-Analysis." In this paper, Freud tells of a woman consulting him after having gone to a young physician for problems with anxiety after a recent divorce. The physician diagnosed the woman's problems as due to a lack of sexual satisfaction and suggested various sexual activities as a remedy. Freud chided the physician for assuming that the woman's primary problem was a lack of information and for believing that by providing this information a cure would follow.

> If knowledge about the unconscious were as important for the patient as people inexperienced in psycho-analysis imagine, listening to lectures or reading books would be enough to cure him. Such measures, however, have as much influence on the symptoms of nervous illness as a distribution of menu-cards in a time of famine has upon hunger. . . . Since, however, psycho-analysis cannot dispense with giving this information, it lays down that this

shall not be done before two conditions have been fulfilled.
First, the patient must, through preparation, himself have
reached *the neighborhood* of what he has repressed, and
secondly, he must have formed a sufficient attachment
(transference) to the physician for his emotional relationship to him to make a fresh flight impossible. [pp. 225–226,
italics added]

By introducing the concept of the patient needing to be
"in the neighborhood," Freud is noting the centrality, among
the principles of clinical technique, of the conscious ego. The
individual must be able to make some connection between
what he is aware of thinking and saying and the therapist's
intervention. No matter how brilliant the therapist's reading
of the unconscious, it is not useful data until it can be
connected to something the patient can be consciously aware
of and find useful. From this perspective, the young physician Freud described did not consider what his patient might
understand, let alone whether she might find his intervention
objectionable. Freud noted that rushing a patient into knowledge of the unconscious would lead the patient to become
antagonistic, and make any further efforts to explore unconscious factors in her symptoms futile.

While few therapists would disagree with the necessity of
one's comments needing to be in the same neighborhood as
the patient's thoughts, my impression is that this is a concept
more honored in the breach. As with that other crucial
concept touching the heart of analytic understanding—resistances—there is what Gray (1982) has aptly described as a
"developmental lag" (p. 621) between our understanding of
the concept at an intellectual level and an affective, clinically
useful one. The patient's fear of and unfamiliarity with
unconscious thoughts and feelings (i.e., resistances), along
with the importance of including the conscious ego in the
working-through process, seem not to have been well integrated within our analytic empathy. Listening to discussions
of the clinical process, one is impressed with how many
interpretations seemed based less on what the patient is

capable of hearing and more on what the therapist is capable of understanding. We too often confuse our ability to read the unconscious and the patient's ability to understand it. We are frequently not clear enough on the distinction between an unconscious communication and our ability to communicate with the patient's unconscious. What the patient can hear, understand, and effectively utilize—let alone the benefits of considering such an approach—are rarely in the foreground of our clinical discussions. Getting to the "real" unconscious fantasy still seems to be our primary therapeutic goal. This appears to be a remnant of the topographic theory we still struggle with.

Greenson is one of those psychotherapists who offered generously of his clinical work. His wisdom and humanity were evident to all those fortunate enough to have heard him present, while his clinical examples elucidate and challenge us. It is in this spirit I present an extended example from Greenson (1967, pp. 299–300) as an introduction to the topic at hand.

In the first year of his analysis, a young man comes into a session angrily denouncing a professor who lectures "without thinking of whether the students can follow." As he continued in this vein, he slipped and said that he hated "to have him treat—I mean, teach me." He then challenges Greenson with the comment, "I suppose you will make something of that." When the patient continues to complain about the professor, Greenson makes a semi-resistance interpretation (i.e., where the resistance is noted but the intent is to not explore it but to get to what is being resisted). Thus, Greenson asks him, "Aren't you trying to run away from your anger towards me?" The patient acquiesces with some expressed doubt but returns with thoughts about feeling sorry for the professor because of rumors that his wife had recently committed suicide. He then returns to complaining about the professor as a "big shot" who "doesn't give a shit for me."

Greenson then intervenes with the following comment: "Aren't you angry with me for going on my vacation next week?" The patient angrily denies this, accusing Greenson of sounding like he looked this up in a book and making a universal analytic comment. Greenson notes his anger but tells the patient his "real" anger is over his vacation. The patient reluctantly agrees and presents some confirmatory data.

From the beginning of this vignette, Greenson seems not to be taking into account what the patient may consciously accept. As with the patient's complaint about his professor, he does not consider "whether the students can follow." The slip that indicates the patient has already made the unconscious connection between his feelings about Greenson and the professor is challenged. Clearly the patient is in an argumentative mood, and connections between Greenson and the professor will not be welcome. It is this resistance that seems most closely available to consciousness. Greenson begins to raise this, but he takes the further step of telling the patient that it is his anger toward Greenson that he is avoiding. Greenson clearly has something in mind, which he finally gets to, when he tells the patient he is angry at Greenson's upcoming vacation. However, there is nothing in the data that suggests that the patient might have any awareness that one might work with, except in the resistance that he is *really* angry at Greenson or that the reason has to do with Greenson's vacation. In bypassing the resistance, the patient's conscious participation is left out of the analysis, except to accept passively the interpretation.

Greenson's explanation for his remarks are that he saw the slip as an indication of the patient's anger, which he refused to consciously accept. This is just the point. *Where* a patient is consciously, and *why* they are there, compose a crucial part of the analytic task. Consciousness is not something to be run roughshod over. Greenson's (1967) explanation is "I believe it is necessary to pursue the resistances until one mobilizes a reasonable ego in the patient" (p. 300). In this, one sees Greenson's tendency to confuse the resistance with the feelings behind the resistance. What he pursued were the patient's feelings of anger. What he did not pursue was the patient's reluctance to make a connection between- Greenson and the professor (i.e., the most observable component of the resistance at that time). Furthermore, for the patient the conscious ego is always the most reasonable one. If we believe a patient is warding off something from consciousness, it is not our task only to bring this to his or her awareness. From the side of the ego, there is a perfectly good reason that it is being warded off, and it is understanding these reasons that is a first step toward conscious acceptance of that which is being warded off.

Thus, this chapter is about the importance of paying attention to what Myerson (1981) has aptly described as the patient's ability to hear our interpretations. It does not appear that this component of the analytic enterprise has been fully integrated into consistent, usable techniques. Herzog (1991) notes that throughout Freud's work, there was no systematic elaboration of consciousness, while Joseph (1987) concludes that Freud did not consider consciousness as particularly worthy of study. Possibly this situation might have been righted if we had access to Freud's missing metapsychological paper on consciousness. However, what we have been left with is a situation in which, at best, we have taken as given the complex, detailed conscious processing that goes on in psychoanalytic work. At worst, the importance of patients' conscious readiness to accept and use our interventions remains relatively ignored. I will first suggest that this developmental lag in integrating a central component of the interpretive process into clinical technique has been, in part, a response to Freud's struggle with the integration of his clinical observations with theory and the relative neglect of the clinical ego in the development of ego psychology. I will then elaborate on the importance of being "in the neighborhood" in the hope that this contribution might be a step in conceptualizing an important but unfinished task in psycho-analysis: the illumination of the role of the ego in the psycho-analytic process.

FREUD, HIS AMBIVALENCE,
AND SOME THAT FOLLOWED

In the paper on "wild" psychoanalysis, Freud (1910a) gently chides the young physician quoted in the paper for his intemperate interpretation. The primary technical error Freud cites is the belief that the patient suffers from a type of ignorance and that by informing the patient one will have cured the neurosis. Freud then highlights the significance of combating the resistances for the success of the analysis. However, toward the end of this article, Freud offers the following surprising caveat:

> "Wild" analysts of this kind do more harm to the cause of psycho-analysis than to individual patients. *I have often found that a clumsy procedure like this, even if at first it produced an exacerbation of the patient's condition, led to a recovery in the end.* Not always but still often. [p. 227, emphasis added]

In this one passage Freud seems to renounce *everything* he has said heretofore. He now comes down on the side of the usefulness of even "clumsy" efforts to bring the unconscious wishes to consciousness, even if the initial effect is deleteri-ous. The importance of being "in the neighborhood" seems now insignificant as an interpretive guideline. The emphasis on the patient's readiness to consciously accept an interpre-tation, and all that it implies, seems now to be disavowed. Freud does this, even though most of what he says previously cautions against taking such an approach, and expresses doubt about the usefulness of such a technique. The reason Freud gives for this turnaround is that he believes the young physician's remarks "forced her attention to the real cause of her trouble, or in that direction, and in spite of all her opposition this intervention of his cannot be without some favorable results" (p. 227). Freud's view now is that bringing the unconscious wishes into awareness has a generally positive, long-term effect on the patient, no matter how the wishes might be brought to the patient's attention. The beneficial outcome is seen as being due to the patient's conscious attention being directed toward the unconscious, even in the face of the resistances. The resistances are reduced to a factor that "[intensifies] the prejudices . . . against the methods of psycho-analysis" (p. 227).

How do we understand these contradictory views? One useful way has recently been described by Lear (1990) as the contradiction between Freud the clinician, "who helped himself to empathic understanding," and Freud the theorist, who "tried to fit psychoanalysis into the scientific image of his day" (p. 5). Freud the clinician understood early on that thoughts were kept out of awareness because of their association with frightening and overwhelming feelings. Therefore, his clinician side understood that patients might be upset with the approaching awareness of unconscious thoughts, because of the unpleasurable affects associated with them. Thus, Freud's earliest clinical description of the ideas that fell prey to censorship were a complex amalgam of feelings and dangers. He says of thoughts that are censored, "[T]hey were all of a distressing nature, calculated to arouse the affects of shame and self-reproach and of psychical pain, and the feeling of being harmed; they were all of a kind one would prefer to have not experienced, that one would rather forget" (Freud 1895, p. 269). This is the Freud who would understand the uselessness of attempting to bring an idea to consciousness until the intense negative feelings surrounding the idea had been ameliorated in some way. This is the Freud who instantly understood the folly of the young physician's remarks. This is the Freud who empathically understood the nature of resistances and kept them at the center of his clinical theory throughout his work.

Freud the theorist held three views in 1910 that are

germane to our discussion. The first of these was that anxiety
was the result of dammed-up libido. The psychic corollary to
this was that only if a wish remained unconscious could it
become pathogenic. The final view was that consciousness
and unconsciousness exist at two different levels of representation, and only by joining these two levels of representation
could an unconscious idea become conscious. The characteristic of consciousness specific to our discussion was that it
was represented by "word presentation." This was in contrast to the unconscious, which was represented by "thing
presentations." In this model, the road to consciousness
involved connecting the thing presentations to word presentations. Thus, Freud the theorist could see how the young
physician could reduce anxiety by putting into words, and
thus making conscious, unfulfilled unconscious wishes.
From this perspective, it was the putting ideas into words
that would remove them from the unconscious and ultimately unblock the dammed-up libido. In short, Freud the
clinician was drawn one way, while Freud the theorist was
drawn in the opposite direction. This distinction is one useful
way to understand the contradictory advice Freud seems to
be giving in this article on the handling of material in
relationship to being "in the neighborhood."

Throughout the rest of Freud's early technical papers
there are references to this same topic, with Freud oscillating
between his clinical and theoretical views. In "The Dynamics
of the Transference," Freud's (1912a) views are dominated
by the necessity of bringing the unconscious thoughts to
consciousness. He suggests that if the patient falls silent, this
stoppage can be eliminated by assuring the patient that he is
holding back thoughts about the therapist. "As soon as this
explanation is given, the stoppage is removed, or the situation is changed from one in which the associations fail into
one in which they are being kept back" (p. 101). In this we
can see that the necessity of the therapist's being in the same
neighborhood as the patient is replaced by a more authoritarian stance. A year later Freud (1913) repeats what was
discussed in the paper on "wild" psychoanalysis. At first he

repudiates the importance of bringing an idea to consciousness without first taking into account how objectionable it
might be to consciousness. He notes, "[T]here was no choice
but to cease attributing to the fact of knowing, in itself, the
importance that had previously been given to it and to place
the emphasis on the resistances which had in the past
brought about the the state of not knowing and which were
still ready to defend that state" (p. 142). However, by the end
of this same page, Freud states, when referring to bringing
repressed material into consciousness, "At first it arouses
resistances, but then, when these have been overcome, it sets
up a process of thought in the course of which the expected
influencing of the unconscious recollection eventually takes
place" (p. 142). This same oscillation occurs in later technical
papers (Freud 1914, 1917a,b).

While Freud did not specifically return to the topic of
being "in the neighborhood" in later papers, the underlying
issues were crucial in later theoretical developments. The
importance of resistances being unconscious was, of course,
a central component in the development of the structural
theory (Freud 1923). Thus, the patient's readiness to accept
interpretations into consciousness, and its relationship to the
unconscious resistances, became a central factor in the structural theory. Freud's (1926) second theory of anxiety came
much closer to capturing his earliest (1895) observations on
those affects associated with keeping thoughts from awareness. However, it was left to others to continue to work on the
clinical significance of this new integration of clinical empathy and psychoanalytic theory.

In A. Freud's (1936) pioneering investigation of the ego,
she notes, "[W]e have realized that large portions of the
ego-institutions are themselves unconscious and require
the help of analysis to become conscious. The result is the
analysis of the ego has assumed a much greater importance
in our eyes" (p. 26). From this perspective, the centrality of
the ego's ability to become aware of its own thought processes was highlighted and continued the thrust of Freud's
attempts to integrate clinical observations with the theory of

the analytic process. Searl's (1936) paper on technique is a clear integration of what was understood to that point on the importance of considering the patient's ability to "hear" interpretations, while anticipating many of the themes Gray was to return to some thirty-five years later. Her description of the importance of taking into account what the patient is capable of becoming aware of, while pointing to the dangers of interpreting "absent content," shows a subtle and complex understanding of the implications for technique of the new ego psychology that was not consistent at the time (see, for example, Reich 1933). Fenichel (1941) succinctly describes the principles under discussion here when he states, "Analysis must always go on in the layers accessible to the ego at the moment. When an interpretation has no effect, one often asks oneself: 'How could I have interpreted more deeply?' But often the question should more correctly be put: 'How could I have interpreted more superficially?' " (p. 44).

However, this line of thinking, which started out in such a promising fashion, soon reached a barrier. There are only scattered references to the concepts implied in the interpretive technique of being "in the neighborhood" over the next thirty years. Kris (1951) states that in second analyses, interpretations that are closer to the surface often lead to significant improvements. Eissler (1965) highlights the importance of interpretations not being isolated from a patient's previous knowledge, while Loewenstein's (1972) concept of identification with the analyst's function is influenced by notions of the importance of autonomous ego functions in the interpretive process. Similar influences can also be seen in the work of Loewald (1960) and Myerson (1960). Why there was this long barren period seems partly related to Freud's ambivalence and partly to issues discussed in the next section. It was not until the work of Paul Gray (1973, 1982, 1986, 1987, 1990a,b, 1991, 1992, 1994)[1] that the centrality

---

1. The entire body of Gray's work will be referred to extensively throughout the chapters. Thus, from this point on, I will give citations only when referring to a specific article.

of the conscious ego in the interpretive process was returned to. No one to that point had approached Gray's meticulous attention to actual techniques in the interpretation of resistances that took into account the conscious ego.

Inspired by the work of Gray, a number of psychotherapists have recently explored an area known as the analytic "surface" (Davison et al 1986, Levy and Inderbitzin 1990, Paniagua 1985). While the emphasis varies slightly, the "surface" generally refers to behaviors that are observable and demonstrable to the patient. In these investigations, the benefits of using the surface, especially in the understanding of resistances, are delved into and elaborated on in a way that gives increasing weight to Gray's work. Thus, we seem to be on the verge of multiple explorations into the role of the conscious ego in the analytic process. Before going further into our own investigation, however, it is important to look at another factor that may have inadvertently hampered psychoanalytic inquiry into the role of the ego in the psychoanalytic process—the development of ego psychology.

HARTMANN'S LEGACY

Possibly no one has captured Heinz Hartmann's place in psychoanalysis as well as Schafer (1970):

> Heinz Hartmann's contributions to psychoanalytic theory (1939, 1960, 1964) rise up before the student of psychoanalysis as a mountain range whose distant peaks with their immense vistas and rarefied atmosphere it is scarcely possible to reach. And yet the student must not only attempt the arduous climb, he must try to get above that range so that he can include Hartmann's work within his own vision of psychoanalysis for that work is not the whole of psychoanalysis, nor can it be the last word on psychoanalytic theory; it is and can only be part of the terrain of scientific psychoanalysis and of science generally. [p. 425]

While agreeing with Smith's (1986) view that we still need time to fully evaluate Hartmann's contributions, one is inevitably drawn to his work with regard to the topic at hand. In fact, Hartmann's work in this area has proven to be both an important contribution and an unwelcome diversion. While stimulating studies that added significant depth to our understanding of subtleties in ego functioning, his emphasis on psychoanalysis as a general psychology may have inadvertently contributed to a diversion from in-depth attention to issues of psychoanalytic technique.

Our views of human behavior were radically changed by Hartmann's perspectives of early ego development and his call for research in child development. His view of the ego as an inborn adaptational structure with predetermined strengths and weaknesses interacting with and affected by an environment that is growth producing or inhibiting, all since shown to be essentially correct by studies of early development, forever changed our view of the infant/child and its earliest development. This, in turn, opened the potential for a new way of understanding patients. To illustrate further, I present a brief example.

A 35-year-old man came for a consultation because he felt his life was passing him by. He did not actually "feel" this but knew from a distance that he had chosen a different life than peers and other family members. While superficially pleasant, he was restricted in what he could allow himself to talk about and in the range of feelings he was able to show. He was able to talk fairly freely while picking and choosing his topics, but any question seemed like an unwelcome intrusion. At these times he would show flashes of anger that quickly faded and remained unobserved. His life was a severely restricted one. He was in a routine job in the family business that was far below what had seemed like his potential at one time. He lived at home, had few friends, and had dated only sporadically since college.

Hartmann's influence looms large in how one might think of this brief vignette from an initial consultation. The restricted nature of the patient's ego functioning is most striking. The need for structure and control both in and out of the consultation is noteworthy, with the flashes of anger a seeming response to threats to his ego integrity. One begins to think of an ego under siege. Questions begin to be raised about the patient's analyzability. Will he be able to tolerate the regressive components of the analytic situation? Will he be able to give up enough control to participate in the process of free association? With such severe, long-term restrictions in his ego functioning, is it not more likely these are due to developmental interferences rather than neurotic conflicts? Were there some interferences in his early "average expectable environment" that may have had a profound influence on early ego functions? Such questions come directly from the work of Hartmann and the psychoanalytic investigations into early development he spawned. The importance of the relationship between the infant/child and its caregiver for psychic survival, as well as a sense of self, cohesion, autonomy, and individuation, along with tolerance for affects and affect regulation, have all been well documented by now (Emde 1988, Mahler et al. 1975, Spitz 1945, Stern 1985, just to name a few).

Hartmann's work set the stage for a subtle approach to the understanding of those factors in the ego that affect acceptance into consciousness. The effect upon conscious receptivity of thoughts to such things as changes in ego states (e.g., fragmentation), regressions in levels of thinking (e.g., from formal operations to preoperational thought), and the degree to which communication is dominated by action are more easily comprehended because of Hartman's work. His inquiries and encouragement of others to map the developmental outline of the ego have had the potential to significantly impact our understanding of what is allowable into consciousness. However, it is not clear this potential has yet been realized. Much of the work of integrating alterations in ego functioning and their effects upon the analytic work have taken place outside the structural theory, most notably in the studies of narcissistic and borderline pathology dominated by the self-psychological and object relations theorists. As Apfelbaum and Gill (1989) conclude, the technical implications of the structural theory seem not to have been noted and implemented. The heart of the structural theory—that in analyzing the ego resistances, one must consider different levels of consciousness—still seems not to be a part of general clinical thinking. To help understand this, I think we need to take a look at Hartmann's work from another dimension.

Many authors have noted that Hartmann's heavy emphasis on metapsychology, which was presented in a way that was removed from clinical data, has had a deleterious effect upon clinical theory and technique (Apfelbaum 1962, Schafer 1970; Shaw 1989). The same might be said, in the short run, for his championing the necessity of studies in child development as a way of understanding ego development. The result has been that Hartmann remains a giant in the psychoanalytic pantheon, but, as Wyman (1989) notes, his ideas seem to have vanished from the literature. While I believe his concepts will prove eminently useable in the long run, it is clear that in the last fifty years psychotherapists have found it difficult to integrate Hartmann's work with clinical technique. The abstractness of his theorizing, while forsaking clinical examples, has left a generation of therapists in awe of Hartmann's intellectual powers, while shaking their heads when considering its relevance to their last patient. The importance of the clinical ego in ego psychology was pushed aside for more abstract theorizing. This was a trend that continued for many years, as noted by Arlow (1975) and Joseph (1975). That Hartmann had a sophisticated clinical view of the ego that took note of such issues as levels of conscious ego and the importance of ego analysis can be glimpsed in the following passage:

> Defenses (typically) not only keep thoughts, images, and instinctual drives out of consciousness, but also prevent their assimilation by means of thinking. When defensive

processes break down, the mental elements defended against and certain connections of these elements become amenable to recollection and reconstruction. Interpretations not only help to regain the buried material, but must also establish correct causal relations, that is, the causes, range of influence, and effectiveness of these experiences in relation to other elements. I stress this here because the theoretical study of interpretation is often limited to those instances which are concerned with emerging memories or corresponding reconstructions. But even more important for the *theory of interpretation* are those instances in which the causal connections of elements, and the criteria for these connections, are established. [Hartmann 1939, p. 63]

One can see the importance for Hartmann, in the interpretive process, of what is allowable into consciousness. He alerts us not only to the significance of the memories associated with repressed trauma but also to the importance of elements of ego functioning associated with defenses and connected to these traumas. He underlines the importance of the expanding awareness of the workings of the conscious ego in the interpretive work and emphasizes the various "mental elements" that are connected to the defenses that become available for entry into consciousness once the defenses become less rigid. We see here the Hartmann who sounds like other voices noted in this chapter who have championed expanding awareness of the conscious ego as a primary interpretive goal (Gray, Kris, Searl). Kafka (1989) also suggests that Hartmann is interested in the shadings of conscious experience.

The quandary posed by Hartmann (1939) for the psychoanalytic clinician is captured in this sentence: "Permit me a digression on the nature of thinking *in the psychoanalytic situation*, in which the predominant object of thought is the subject himself" (p. 62). The fact that Hartmann considered thinking about the psychoanalytic situation as a "digression" was evident in his theorizing. This approach hampered the translation of ego psychology into a viable component of clinical psychoanalysis. While ego analysis was championed in print, its translation into understandable, workable approaches in the clinical situation lagged behind. Thus, the clinical issue of availability to consciousness as one consideration in the therapist's interpretive stance, which began in conflict between Freud the empathic observer and Freud the scientist, once again was obscured behind Hartmann the theoretician. Hartmann's legacy is that while he opened a window to the possibility of subtleties in understanding of ego functions, the shade remained drawn on the clinical ego.

IMPORTANCE OF BEING "IN THE NEIGHBORHOOD"

The centrality of being in the neighborhood for the analytic process is emphasized in Gray's pioneering work on resistance analysis, in which he has championed the importance of the conscious ego in the analytic process. In a twist of Freud's adage, Gray (1990a) points to the usefulness of looking at the goals of the psychoanalytic process in terms of "where unconscious ego was, conscious ego shall be" (p. 1095). In a series of articles over the last two decades, Gray has given us a clear methodology for analyzing the unconscious ego resistances while helping patients become aware of their mental activity. His emphasis has been on helping patients gain a greater access to consciousness of those unconscious ego activities that lead to resistances. For Gray, a successful interpretation has, as one component, a direction of the patient to something *he or she can understand* in spite of ongoing resistances. He asserts (Gray 1990a) that by including the conscious ego in our interpretive stance, we encourage and strengthen more mature ego functioning. Finally, Gray (1986) believes that the results of treatment are dependent upon the degree to which we have not bypassed ego functions.

The significance of the patient's conscious awareness of his own thoughts is also seen in the work of Anton Kris (1982,

1983, 1990, 1992).[2] Kris, who has considered the conscious ego from a somewhat different perspective, uses the method of free association as the frame of his analytic perspective and suggests there are inherent satisfactions with freedom of associations. His conception of a pathological process, within the context of the analytic setting, involves an inhibition of the pleasure in being able to conceptualize and *become aware of one's thought processes*. Thus, using interferences with the method of free association as a basis of pathology, Kris takes the position that a definition of health needs to take into account the ability to become *consciously* aware of one's thoughts with a corresponding decrease in unconscious resistances to this process.

In the work of both Gray and Kris one sees a view of pathology, which is defined within the analytic process, as an interference with the ability to become *conscious of one's thought processes*. Both use consciousness as a basis of understanding resistances. A corollary of this from the interpretive side is that the therapist's task is to help make conscious the unconscious resistances in a way that allows patients to have greater access to their mental life. To do this is to keep in mind at all times what the patient can become conscious of. As Gray (1986) suggests, "The interpretive task is to estimate sensitively the patient's ability to comprehend, in order to make a formulation that is not too superficial, yet does not stimulate more reactive defenses" (p. 253). In this same vein, he notes his belief that "[t]he effectiveness with which patients can use their capacity for observing ego activities depends primarily on the nature of the burden the analyst's interventions place on them" (p. 253). This burden can be decreased by focusing on the unconscious resistances via the patient's communications and interferences with the free-associative method. By directing one's comments to the "neighborhood" the patient presently occupies in a way that demystifies the basis of our remarks, we go a long way toward

---

2. Kris's work will also be cited extensively, and thus only specific citations will be noted.

inviting conscious participation in the therapeutic process.

What has not been sufficiently emphasized in the literature to this point are the problems inherent in *not* being "in the neighborhood." Simply put, given the centrality of the unconscious ego resistances in the analytic process, it is futile to be anyplace else. Thus, if one primary purpose of a resistance is to keep thoughts and feelings out of awareness, then not to take into account what can be allowed into awareness when making an intervention is to risk our comments falling on deaf ears, at best, and potentially arousing more resistances. Since Freud's (1926) elaboration of his second theory of anxiety, it has been clear that resistances are, in part, the ego's response to some experienced danger or threat. Thus, if a resistance is in operation, it indicates that the patient is experiencing his or her thoughts or feelings as a danger. The purpose of the resistance is to keep the dangerous thought or feeling from awareness. The particular type of resistance is an adaptation, from an earlier time, to this threat. Interventions that do not respect the patient's resistance to certain thoughts and feelings becoming conscious will be either irrelevant or potentially overwhelming. This basic component of the analytic process has been muddled by our developmental lag (Gray 1982) in understanding the resistances (see also Busch 1992, Schafer 1983).

A different perspective on the futility of interpreting outside the neighborhood is presented in the work of G. Klein (1976). Klein shows that the basic purpose of any defensive process is to take the meaning out of behavior that is drive dominated. Thus, the person with exhibitionistic wishes, for example, is aware only of feeling self-conscious that people are staring at her, while someone in the throes of an oedipal rivalry knows only about his discomfort around older authority figures. Wishes have an active, ongoing influence on behavior, while the individual has no understanding of the behavior or feeling associated with the wish. Thus, the critical accomplishment of defenses is the establishment of a gap between behavior and conscious comprehension of that behavior. The meaning of wishes can be lived out without any conscious understanding. The individual who can "barely" go out in public due to vague feelings of shame and embarrassment when others are looking is living out an ongoing expression of exhibitionistic wishes. The crucial component of the defense is that the individual can live out the wish without any conscious comprehension. One important goal of an interpretation, then, is to *fill out gaps in meaning* (and not necessarily gaps in memory). The bridge must be made between unconscious wishes acted upon in behaviors and their conscious meanings, along with the reasons for their being kept apart (i.e., the resistances). Until such a bridge is made, behaviors remain unresponsive to feedback, and thus not modifiable. The exhibitionist cannot think of leaving the house while fervidly believing she is avoiding pain and discomfort by staying home. The conscious understanding that behaviors have meaning, that there are reasons for our keeping a gap between the behavior and its meaning, and finally of what the behaviors mean become the significant steps in a patient's obtaining understanding of his or her behavior. By not taking into account the patient's conscious readiness to grasp the meaning of his or her behavior, we are missing one of the basic points of the defenses, which is to keep meanings outside awareness. Only by gradually making behaviors consciously meaningful can we hope to modify the basic defensive structure. Defenses are instituted in such a manner that wishes can be lived out without comprehension. With our interpretations we hope to bring meaning to this lack of comprehension, while increasing comprehension. Without participation of the patient's conscious ego, we subvert our own goals.

A more subtle, and potentially more insidious, problem is the enfeebling and undermining of the ego that occurs when the patient's conscious awareness is not taken into account. This can be seen most frequently in what Searl (1936) calls the interpretation of "absent content" (i.e., the interpretation of a fantasy or feeling that the patient is unaware of), an example of which can be seen in the Greenson vignette cited

earlier. In outlining some of the problems with such interpretations, Searl (1936) notes:

> If on the other hand, we say to a patient, "You are thinking
> so and so," "You have such and such a fantasy," and so on,
> we give him no help about his inability to know that for
> himself, and leave him to some extent *dependent on the*
> *analyst for all such knowledge.* If we add "The nature of
> this thought or fantasy explains your difficulty in knowing
> it for yourself," we still leave the patient with increased
> understanding related to a particular type of thought and
> fantasy only, and imply "One must know the thought or
> fantasy first before one can understand the difficulty about
> knowing it." *The dynamics about the patient's disability*
> *to find his own way have been comparatively untouched*
> if the resistance was more than the thinnest of crusts, and
> will therefore still be at work to some extent and in some
> form whatever the change brought about by the absent
> content. [pp. 478–479, italics added]

By including the conscious ego in our interventions, we
encourage the patient to take a more active role in treatment.
This approach is in contrast to those interpretations geared
toward absent content which, as Searl demonstrates, enforce
a passivity on the patient. Such interpretations encourage a
belief in the therapist's omniscience, while stimulating the
patient's omnipotent fantasies and reinforcing a belief in
magical thinking. Searl's work also suggests that by interpreting content outside of a patient's awareness, we may
participate in a bypassing of resistances to independent
self-analysis (i.e., the dynamics of the patient's inability to
find his or her own way). This fear and/or distortion of the
ability to observe one's own thought processes is a significant
resistance in every analysis, but it has been obscured by
gaps in our understanding of ego analysis. How frequently
have we heard about instances in what seem to be relatively
successful treatments in their final stages in which the
patient "associates" and the therapist "interprets"? The
patient's participation in the process of analyzing is too

infrequently analyzed, partly because we are not paying attention to the nature of what would be most helpful to the patient in understanding the analytic process. Is it the understanding of the patient's unconscious fantasies, or is it the increasingly conscious awareness of one's own thought processes and the barriers to this awareness? I do not in any way rule out the centrality of understanding unconscious conflicts and the resulting compromise formations in symptom resolution. Inevitably, all resistances to self-awareness are intertwined with persistent fantasies that dominate unconscious thoughts. It is simply a question of the best way to show these to the patient so that the analytic process is furthered.

The therapist's task is a daunting one. Translating the patient's action thoughts while understanding unconscious components of a communication from the side of the id, ego, and superego is difficult enough. Communicating this to the patient in a way he or she can understand, while also being relevant to concerns the patient is aware of struggling with, is a never-ending test of the therapist's cognitive and empathic abilities. While recently listening to a colleague interpret, for what seemed like the umpteenth time, a patient's passive homosexual wishes as a defense against his active strivings, I thought of our tendency to interpret (and if the patient is not able to use what we say, then to interpret again) as being like trying to give directions to someone who doesn't speak our language. Invariably in these situations we tend to speak louder and slower, as if by doing this the foreigner will understand better. Our repetitions of the absent unconscious fantasy in its various forms has the same quality. By continuing to focus on absent content, we may be engaging in a process that undermines the ego, while, via our empathic disruption with what the patient is capable of hearing, we may increase the sense of danger and thus intensify resistances.

I have focused to this point on the dangers of not being "in the neighborhood." Yet the question remains as to what the benefits are of including the conscious ego as part of the

intervention process. Inviting the patient's more active participation supports the enlistment of certain ego pleasures
that have not been well integrated into psychoanalytic technique. These pleasures are well known to observers of children. Klein (1976) outlines some of the pleasures associated
with ego activities as functioning (the activity itself is pleasurable), effectance (changing a course of action through
one's behavior), and synthesis (establishing a sense of order
and wholeness). These are similar to ego activities noted by
Erikson (1963) and White (1963) as well as many others. In a
similar vein, Emde (1988), in reviewing the early childhood
research, concludes that two of the most basic motivations
for behavior are activity and self-regulation. It is clear in
observational research that from very early on we are driven
by, and find pleasure in, a number of ego activities. These
have been called by various names over the years (e.g., a
drive for competence, a need for mastery, etc.), and further
clarity is still needed. However, what cannot be doubted are
the active ego needs and pleasure in them. In our daily
analytic work, we are much more impressed with how the
ego becomes compromised by resistances and unconscious
fantasies. Stereotypical, repetitive restrictions in characteristic ego activities, for much of an analysis, are the observational fare of most therapists. The numbing effect of an ego
caught in conflict should not be confused with its potential
resilience. We should not, in a countertransference acting
out, treat our adult patients as cognitively impoverished, as
they appear when a threatened ego is temporarily restricted.
With a respectful eye on the conscious ego and its pleasures,
we can point to the way ego functioning becomes compromised by conflict, which thus removes significant pleasure in
ego activities. Working with patients in this way often leads
them to a feeling they have "found a part of themselves" or
they consider their thoughts more "their own."

   Gray (1982) observed that an important distinguishing
element among therapists is their *"forms of attention"* (p.
621) during the analysis. This can be said both about the type
of the material listened for and how the therapist communi-

cates his or her understanding to the patient. In terms of the latter, one hears variations in style—from the therapist who always seems to "assert" what is going on at any moment in the analysis, to those who seem to believe that it is only the patient who can come to his own understanding and thus say almost nothing. Gray's method of sharing the data that led to his conclusion invites the patient's conscious ego to participate in the process. It not only has the advantages associated with including the conscious ego in the analytic process but also helps focus in a minute way on resistances to the process. This is essential in analyzing resistances to the self-analytic function, which seems crucial for posttermination success.

Weinshel (1984) suggests that a useful way of distinguishing among therapists is that there are those who focus on the goal of analysis, and there are those who focus on the analytic work. Different ways of interpreting to patients highlight these differences. Inherent within the position of the therapist who "asserts" interpretations is the goal of bringing unconscious thoughts to consciousness. This therapist would thus be working within a topographic model in which the therapeutic benefit of analysis is viewed in terms of goals. By sharing with patients the reasons for our inferences as well as our inferences, we are emphasizing the process. We are saying to our patients, "In your use of the method, we can learn such and such from what you are saying." It isn't that there aren't goals with such a method; it is that the goals are reached by focusing on the method. Implicit in one's approach toward interventions there are also hidden assumptions about the nature of the analytic process. The approach I have been suggesting is concisely captured in Gill's (1954) felicitous, oft-quoted comment that we still recognize our friends after they have successfully completed an analysis. If one believes that the work of analysis centers around continuing the work of analysis rather than obliteration of conflict, then including the conscious ego in a variety of ways becomes a necessary component of the process.

In follow-up studies of completed psychoanalyses by

Schlessinger and Robbins (1983) there are clear indications that core conflicts are not dissolved. Instead, what one sees from posttermination interviews is an emergence of, and then a working on, issues that were central in the analysis. Under periods of stress (such as with the stimulation of the ever-ready transference fantasies arising in a posttermination interview), old conflicts arise, but this time to be handled far more swiftly and with less disruption. Analysis obliterates neither conflict nor the character patterns of resistances and gratifications surrounding conflict. Instead, what analysis accomplishes, from this one perspective, is help in making accessible to consciousness the resistances fed by anxiety and accompanied by an array of unconscious fantasies and traumas. Analysis allows for a greater access to consciousness of these myriad components of conflict, which allows for more rapid resolution of the immediate stresses via self-analysis. This capacity for self-analysis, rather than obliteration of conflict, is one of the prime benefits one sees from successfully completed analyses, according to Schlessinger and Robbins (1983). As Calef (1982) notes, the outcome of analysis may be most influenced by whether the patient has been able to identify with its process.

Finally, it is at least important to note there are resistances to including the conscious ego in the interpretive process that lead both the therapist and patient away from the importance of being "in the neighborhood." Gray (1982) and I (Busch 1992) have commented on the magnetism of unconscious fantasies for the therapist in resistances to analyzing the resistances, and the same can be said here. Universal trends from childhood also tend to pull the patient toward a more regressive relationship in which the patient "associates" and the therapist interprets. These can include such wishes as the desire to remain in a dependent position in relationship to an omniscient, omnipotent figure; the narcissistic pleasure of being at the center of another's attention who is observing and attempting to make sense of whatever one is saying; and the pleasure of letting one's mind go without believing there is the need for *any* structure or

control. Furthermore, there are regressions in ego functioning concomitant with the development of the transference neurosis that preclude the patient from observing his or
her own thoughts. For example, an individual functioning
under the influence of preoperational thought feels need to
justify his reasonings to others. Neither does he search for
contradictions in his logic. He cannot reconstruct a chain of
reasoning that he has just passed through; he thinks but he
cannot think about his own thinking. When a patient is in
such a state, his or her thoughts are closer to actions, and he
or she does not recognize there is a "neighborhood" to be in.
Thus, when we observe these resistances to conscious aware-
nees (whether in the form of an ego regression or regression
in wish), we need to analyze them as we would any resistance. The danger lies in bypassing an important impediment to self-analysis (i.e., the inability to become aware of
one's thought process or the wish not to become aware). This
takes on added importance when we consider Loewald's
(1971) suggestion that part of the curative process in psychoanalysis rests on experiences now coming under the influence of higher-level ego functions that were previously not
available to consciousness.

FREE ASSOCIATION

Freud's method of free association, labeled the *fundamental rule* of psychoanalysis in 1912 but already considered part of his psychoanalytic technique by 1892, remained unchanged as a technical precept from its elaboration in "The Interpretation of Dreams":

> We therefore tell him that the success of the psychoanalysis depends on his noticing and reporting whatever comes into his head and not being misled, for instance, into suppressing an idea because it strikes him as unimportant or irrelevant or because it seems to him meaningless. He must adopt a completely impartial attitude to what occurs to him, since it is precisely his critical attitude which is responsible for his being unable, in the ordinary course of things, to achieve the desired unravelling of his dream or obsessional idea or whatever it may be. [1900, p. 101]

In listening to colleagues present clinical data, it does not appear as if significant changes have occured in the *intent* or

tone of the instructions given to patients since Freud's original description. While the words may be different, Moore and
Fine's (1990) description of free association some eighty-five
years later defines the expectations for the patient as essentially the same.

> The patient in psychoanalytic treatment is asked to ex-
> press in words all thoughts, feelings, wishes, sensations,
> images, and memories, without reservation, as they spon-
> taneously occur. This requirement is called the funda-
> mental rule of psychoanalysis. In following the rule, the
> patient must often overcome conscious feelings of embar-
> rassment, fear, shame, and guilt. His or her cooperation is
> motivated in part by knowledge of the purpose for which he
> or she is in analysis—to deal with conflicts and overcome
> problems. [p. 78]

It is difficult to know what to make of Lichtenberg and
Galler's (1987) survey of therapists' presentation of the fundamental rule. A skewed sample, giving variable responses
(in terms of detail), can only give one an impressionistic view
of some therapists' current perception of how they practice.
While the authors are impressed with the diversity of responses they received, I am impressed with their similarities
to the guidelines suggested by Freud. With some exceptions,
the numbers of which are difficult to determine, the *intent* of
the instructions often remains the same: "I hope you will
express yourself as freely as possible because the more you
can do so, the more likely it is that we will be able to work
usefully. . . . I'd like you to tell me as fully as you can
everything as it enters your mind and I will try to help you as
best as I can" (pp. 64–65). Lichtenberg and Galler's charac-
terization of the tone of the guidelines given to patients as
"gentle exhortation" (p. 63) captures a current dilemma for
many therapists. The strident nature of Freud's view of the
method of free association seems alien—thus the "gentle"
component. Yet we still believe it necessary to "exhort" our
patients to hold back as little as possible. One does get the
impression from this study, and from informal discussions

with colleagues, that subtle changes in the method of free association are being made. However, the reasons for such changes and their implications for technique have not been made explicit. This is especially important in that, at present, most therapists would agree with Kranzer's assessment that "[F]ree association remains the essential instrument of psychoanalytic investigative techniques" (Panel 1971, p. 104) or Kris's (1990b) observation that "free association is the hallmark of psychoanalytic treatment conducted by analysts of every stripe" (p. 26).

This chapter, then, is in the spirit of the conclusion from a panel on this topic that ended with the thoughts "Free Association, so basic to the science of psychoanalysis, is far from being a closed book . . . and that despite the further delineation of the conceptualization of it, thus far we are still on the threshold of the exploration of its many mysteries" (Panel 1971, p. 109). It is the contention of this chapter that conceptual contradictions are buried in the method of free association as currently practiced, which lead to confusion in the method and goals of psychoanalysis.

Recent advances in understanding the ego have given us the potential for a method of free association subtly different from Freud's. However, these different views, and reasons they are necessary, have not been fully explicated. Thus, for some my argument will have a familiar ring to it, in that older and newer models of the method have been blended together and differences between them have become blurred. However, I will explore the distinction between Freud's view of the method, and the problematic view of the psychoanalytic process it fosters, and some current views of psychoanalytic technique rooted in the structural model that have important implications for the method of free association.

FREE ASSOCIATION AND RESISTANCE ANALYSIS

Freud's discovery and elucidation of free association stems from a time when he viewed anxiety as the result of dammed-up libido, and his model of the mind was the topographical one. These views cast a long shadow over the method of free association. The purpose of free association was to get out in the open something that was unconsciously being held back. While Freud understood and appreciated resistances and wrote about them, at times with a clinical sensitivity enviable even today (see Freud 1895, p. 269), his technical handling of resistances relied primarily on suggestion, education, and the influence accrued to the therapist via the positive transference, to overcome resistances. The method of free association as first developed was geared toward *overcoming* and not *understanding* the resistances. Thus, in his instructions to patients Freud (1913) included the following injunctions against holding anything back:

> You will be tempted to say to yourself that this or that is irrelevant here, or is quite unimportant, or nonsensical, so that there is no need to say it. You must never give in to these criticisms, but must say it in spite of them—indeed, you must say it precisely *because* you feel an aversion to doing so. Later on you will find out and learn to understand the reason for this injunction, which is really the only one you have to follow. . . . Finally, never forget that you have promised to be absolutely honest, and never leave anything out because, for some reason or other, it is unpleasant to say it. [p.135]

This recommendation was repeated in 1923: "They were to communicate these ideas to the physician even if they felt objections to doing so, if, for instance, the thoughts seemed too disagreeable, too senseless, too unimportant or irrelevant" (p. 195). Freud's view of the technical significance of this prohibition against holding thoughts back is captured in the following statement: "It is very remarkable how the whole task becomes *impossible* if a reservation is allowed at any single place" (1913, p. 135, italics added). On another occasion, referring to the prohibition against holding thoughts back, Freud (1917c) referred to it as his "sacred rule" (p. 288).

Thus, it becomes clear that the very essence of the method of free association was geared toward overcoming and not analyzing resistances. When a resistance developed, the patient was instructed to push on in spite of it. Freud saw the work of analysis as "impossible" as long as resistances were in evidence. This belief held in spite of the fact that he saw resistances as an inevitable part of the analysis. I believe this is another crucial component in the developmental lag of integrating resistance analysis into clinical technique that Gray (1982) and I (Busch 1992) have discussed, while also contributing to a critical attitude towards resistances on the part of many therapists. While therapists generally agree that resistances are the ego's response to distressing affect, as first described by Freud (1923, 1926), and that resistance analysis is a cornerstone of the psychoanalytic method, *our technique of analyzing as expressed in our instructions to patients is geared toward bypassing the importance of these affects and the ego's responses to them.* This view seems to be a factor in why so many therapists persist in seeing their purpose as "getting out" the strangulated affect or unconscious fantasy in spite of seemingly sophisticated views of the resistances (e.g., Greenson 1967, pp. 299–300). The basic mission of analysis, as defined by the original intent of the method of free association, is to have the patient hold back as little as possible. Although this contradiction exists (i.e., we believe the patient should not hold back anything while considering it crucial to work with those reasons he or she inevitably holds back), confusion over goals and methods of analysis must exist. We cannot continue to ask the patient to say what comes to mind no matter how painful without acknowledging the impossibility of the task and the importance of understanding the reasons for its impossibility. Our understanding of resistances dictates that instruction in the method of free association needs to be updated.

Until recently, there have been few critiques of the method of free association. As Mahoney (1979) notes, many of Freud's original ideas on this subject get "reiterated in the psychoanalytic literature with very little advance beyond them" (p. 163). Kris (1992) observes that even through the height of the ego-psychological approach to psychoanalytic technique, insight remained intertwined with the lifting of repression and the topographic notion of making the unconscious conscious. Thus, the method of free association, when emphasizing the pushing away of resistances so that the unconscious could be observed, was quite compatible with this approach. An exception was the work of Loewenstein (1963), who notes, as Freud does, that the "possibility of complying with such a request is severely limited" (p. 455) and quietly changes the focus of the associative process when he suggests that "the patient is expected to observe and express emerging thoughts as well as *his reluctance to perceive or verbalize them*" (p. 454, emphasis added). With this additional focus, the resistance is brought to center stage in the associative process. The patient's focus is equally on the emerging thoughts and those barriers to thought. However, Loewenstein (1963) does not note the slight but significant alteration in perspective, seemingly because of his belief in Freud's "insistence on the importance of analyzing resistances" (p. 254). While this observation is correct from one perspective, as noted earlier, Freud's view of analyzing resistances relied heavily on suggestion and persuasion.

A number of therapists have argued that directing the patient to hold nothing back exerts a type of superego burden that the patient cannot meet (Blum 1981, Epstein 1976, Kanzer 1972). That the patient's attempt to meet the demands of free association was doomed to failure was well known to Freud. Thus, in discussing free association Freud (1913) states, "Later, under the dominance of the resistances, obedience to it weakens, and there comes a time in every analysis when the patient disregards it" (p. 135). In presenting free association as a demand on the patient to say everything that comes to mind, without any stated modifications regarding the difficulties of the task we are asking of them, we will likely contribute to the opposite effect than intended. We are consigning the patient's efforts to inevitable failure, with each individual's response based upon his particular psychology (some patients will become secretive; some rebellious; some passive; etc.). This is not to say that giving the correct instructions will do away with reactions to the associative process. However, there are important differences between the reality of being asked to comply with an impossible task and a fantasy that this is what is being asked.

A fresh approach to the method of free association is found in the work of A. Kris and Gray. Instead of seeing resistances as a barrier to free association, they see free association as a method by which resistances can become the centerpiece of the analytic process. For Kris, "the first aim of the method is to help diminish through understanding the *unconscious* restrictions that limit the associations" (1990a, p. 27). The key component of this approach is that "through understanding," the inevitable resistances are worked on, with the goal of increasing the patient's conscious acceptance of his or her thought. No longer are the resistances an impediment that makes treatment "impossible." Instead, as Gray notes, of central importance is to help patients become aware of unconscious ego resistances that serve long outmoded adaptive functions.

In an attempt to correct the strikingly absent methodology for working with resistances, both authors focus on the *process* of free association rather than its hidden content. The heart of their technique involves listening for the moment in the associations when a resistance is in operation. Gray has likened it to an apple picker watching a conveyer belt for bad apples. One's attention is on the flow of material, looking for some change that indicates that the flow of thoughts has been blocked. This is the moment of the resistance and the point at which the analysis of the resistances begins.

The advantages of this method over searching for the hidden content (i.e., by the therapist's either directing the patient to describe what he or she is holding back or interpreting what was not said) have been known for some time (see Searl 1936), and recently brought to our attention again by Gray. In essence, investigating the resistances to free associations rather than circumventing them has been shown to be an ego-strengthening rather than -weakening technique. While there are significant differences between Kris and Gray in their techniques for investigating the resistances and in the specifics of how they see this process helping the patient, both have given psychotherapists a way of thinking about working with free associations that corrects one of our oldest methodological inconsistencies and fits with our understanding of the workings of the mind as modified by our knowledge of the unconscious resistances. Before their work, therapists had to resolve how they could implore patients to follow the basic rule while also believing that working through resistances was a cornerstone of analytic technique. This has had a profound effect on the methods and goals of psychoanalysis.

Gray's (1986) instructions, which include the expectation that resistances to the method of free association will occur, could serve as a useful model for most therapists. He makes clear that he is describing an attempt at free association, since interferences regularly occur. He emphasizes that it is just these interferences to verbalizing one's observations that need to be studied because they point the way to what is not accesible and what will ultimately contribute to the patient's problems that brought him or her to treatment.

With this addition to the basic rule, conveyed in whatever language and with whatever timing the therapist deems best, we tilt the method of free association toward the study of resistances. Kris (personal communication) suggests that "instructions are designed to reduce *reluctances*, but to highlight *resistances*, not to circumvent them." This will not solve the problem of what Gray (1982) has called therapists' resistances to resistance analysis, but it is an attempt to correct what is an ongoing difficulty for many therapists— that is, integrating the structural model into clinical technique.

SELF-REFLECTION AND FREE ASSOCIATION

The role of the patient's interest in and capacity for thinking about his or her own thought processes has been confounded from the beginning of the method of free association. Freud's (1900) stated view was that *reflecting* on one's thoughts, in contrast to *observing* them (i.e., like a passenger on a train), was antithetical to the method of free association.

> I have noticed in my psycho-analytic work that the whole frame of mind of a man who is reflecting is totally different [from] that of a man who is observing his own psychical processes. In reflection there is one more psychical activity at work than in the most attentive self-observation, and this is shown amongst other things by the tense looks and wrinkled forehead of a person pursuing his reflections as compared with the restful expression of a self observer. In both cases attention must be concentrated, but the man who is reflecting is also exercising his *critical* faculty; this leads him to reject some of the ideas that occur to him after perceiving them, to cut short others without following the trains of thought which they would open up to him. [pp. 101–102]

Yet shortly after rejecting a reflective mode of thought as an interference to free association, Freud (1900) in quoting a letter written by the poet and philosopher Schiller, supports the necessity of self-reflection in order to make sense of associations.

> Looked at in isolation a thought may seem very trivial or very fantastic; but it may be made important by another thought that comes after it, and, in conjunction with thoughts that seem equally absurd, it may turn out to form a most effective link. *Reason cannot form any opinion upon all this unless it retains the thought long enough to look at it in connection with others.* On the other hand, where there is a creative mind, Reason—so it seems to

me—relaxes its watch upon the gates, and the ideas rush in pell-mell, *and only then does it look them through and examine them in a mass.* [p. 103, italics added].

Here, in quoting Schiller, Freud is saying that observation of one's thoughts is really not enough. *In order to make anything of one's observations, the observations need to be observed.* Freud's concern over the critical component of reflection involves the first level of observations (i.e., free associations), not the further reflections on the observations. Yet, given Freud's theoretical views and clinical experience at the time, it is not surprising that he would come to focus on the freedom of the free associations as the key to symptom removal. Thus, his instructions to patients, as noted in the previous section, are geared toward as little self-reflection as possible. This approach persisted in spite of the fact that Freud (1917c) recognizes some patients can associate perfectly well, yet nothing ever comes of it.

While Freud championed the importance of the patient's associations, the significance of the patient's contemplation, reflection, or observation of his or her associations remained in murkier territory—and still remains there. As I have mentioned elsewhere (Busch 1992), the primary model for many analyses is that the patient associates, and the therapist *observes* and interprets. The patient's interest and ability to reflect back on thoughts, or his or her resistance to doing so, seem not to be a common part of the analytic field.[1] Yet, as we shall see, the capacity for the patient to observe his

---

1. While agreeing with the thrust of Spacal's (1990) article on free association, I believe his description of the method as one of self-observation has its limitations. The method is designed to help patients become aware they are having thoughts (and resistances to these thoughts), and, as Kris (1982) notes, one of the goals of psychoanalysis is to increase the freedom of associations. In this sense, it is designed to increase observation of a part of the self (i.e., thoughts). This is only a beginning step in a larger process of seeing thoughts as having a coherent meaning. I believe it is this second process that fits the spirit of the term *self-observation.*

or her thoughts is seen as an important, yet neglected, part of the outcome of psychoanalytic treatment.

Sterba's (1934) classic paper on the fate of the ego in psychoanalysis brought therapists' attention to the significance of the patient's observations of the ongoing analytic process. He describes what he calls a "dissociation" in the ego that develops during the analytic process and becomes the *sine qua non* of the success of the analysis. Freud (1932) had already suggested this when he described the ego's capacity to take itself as an object and observe itself, while also characterizing the goal of psychoanalysis as widening the ego's field of perception. Sterba states that the "dissociation" occurs when, via the therapist's interpretations, an alliance is formed with the ego that helps dissociate it from instinctual and repressive forces. The fate of the analysis is seen as resting with experiences in which, "the subject's consciousness shifts from the center of affective experience to that of intellectual contemplation" (p. 121). According to Friedman (1992), "Sterba saw it as a variant of the normal, characteristically human capacity of reflection, the sort of thing a Piagetian might describe as operating upon one's operations, or a philosopher might refer to as abstracting from one's abstractions, or a man in the street might say amounts to looking hard at oneself" (p. 3). It is a process in which the patient steps back from the experience of the analysis (i.e., his or her thoughts and feelings) and reflects on it—just the type of analytic experience Freud seemed ambivalent about.

Surprisingly, Sterba's concept remains "dissociated" from the theory of the psychoanalytic process. It is one of those concepts that, while generally accepted as a necessary component of the process, is not fully integrated into our theory. Friedman (personal communication) calls it "an unscrutinized presupposition of the psychoanalytic procedure." The centrality of the concept is captured poetically by Gardner (1983) when he states, "Every patient and every psychoanalyst, the first and each after, has struggled and will struggle between aims to advance self inquiry and aims to obstruct it" (p. 8).

While Friedman (1992) points out that self-reflection is often confused with the "therapeutic alliance," there seems to be a generally accepted developmental line from self-reflection to self-analysis. The essence of this perspective is caught in Kantrowitz and colleagues' (1990) statement that "[w]e define self-analysis as the capacity to *observe and reflect* upon one's own behaviors, feelings, or fantasy life in a manner that leads to understanding the meaning of that phenomenon in a new light" (pp. 639–640, emphasis added). Others have seen this capacity as an important one that develops during the analysis and as a criterion for termination (Gaskill 1980, Novick 1982). Yet, for the most part, comments in the literature on the significance of the patient's capacity to reflect on his or her association are presented as sidelights to other issues and are not addressed head-on. For example, Loewenstein (1963) notes, "Not only does the analyst pay equal attention to id, ego, and superego manifestations, but even the patient is expected to *observe and express* his emerging thoughts as well as his reluctance to perceive or verbalize them" (p. 178, italics added). At a later point Loewenstein (1972) writes, "What the patient learns from his analyst is to allow certain thoughts to become available to himself, and to look at them from a point of view acquired from the analyst" (p. 221).

Similar thoughts (i.e., on the significance of a split-off ego for the success of the analytic process) have been expressed by others (Fenichel 1941, A. Freud 1936, Greenson 1967, Kris 1956a,b, Nunberg 1955). Weinshel (1984) highlights the significance of the development of self-reflection to the analytic process in this way: "I would suggest that this organization and these structures—the psychoanalytic process—remain as permanent products of the reasonably successful analysis and that their presence is reflected most immediately and most tangentially in the operation of a more effective and more 'objective' capacity for self observation" (p. 82). He bolsters his argument for the importance of this development (as Kantrowitz et al. does), by citing data on follow-ups of successfully completed analyses that indicate the importance of the internalization of an observing function. Sonnenberg's (1991) description of his ongoing analysis supports this view. However, for Weinshel, as for those analysts who have considered the subject before him, the development of the observing capacity is not so much a part of the analysis as a *side effect*. It is most frequently written about as a function of an identification with the therapist, or the work of the analysis, or the process of analysis, but not as an integral part of the analytic work.

The significance of self-observation *as part of* the analytic process has been most clearly articulated by Gray. In elaborating on Sterba's early views, Gray (1986) sees self-observation developing as a result of systematic analysis, akin to analysis of the freedom of the patient's thoughts.

Thus Gray views self-observation not only as an important goal of analysis but as the focus of the analysis. Following the work of A. Freud (1936), he treats the ego as the seat of observation. He reminds us that the ego is under the sway of various forces that influence how a patient does and does not think about him- or herself. Thus, the primary focus of Gray's technique is toward helping patients observe their unconscious defensive activity designed to keep thoughts out of awareness. By staying closely attuned to conflicts in action that are observable to the patient, Gray works toward strengthening and giving greater autonomy to those ego functions involved with observation and thought. This approach is in contrast to those techniques that rely primarily on the therapist's empathic or intuitive reading of the unconscious, which bypasses the ego's participation in the process except to admire the therapist's observational capacities. He deplores the fact that as a result of such an approach, the ego's role in bringing about resistance is unlikely to be explored, leaving the capacity for self-observation seriously weakened.

Using Freud's later model of the mind, Gray has shown the significance of the ego's self-observational capacities for the analytic process in resistance analysis and the growth of autonomy via strengthening those observational abilities. The resistances Gray highlights are those seen in the moment-to-moment observation of the patient's associations. A typical example cited by Gray is when there is a break in the associative narrative after the emergence of a disturbing thought. Gray then helps the patient observe the resistances in action and also understand the causes for the resistances. This is one form of expanding the ego's observational capacities.

Important, also, is the analysis of resistances to thoughts as meaningful (i.e., self-observation as a method for self-analysis). Therapists have long been aware of the dynamic significance of resistances to self-analysis (e,g., self-analysis as a dangerous challenge to the therapist or as a capitulation; thoughts representing feces that can be presented but not touched or that are presented to the therapist for admiration). However, there is a way of thinking, characteristic of an ego caught in conflict, that ensures that the patient remains oblivious to thoughts about his or her thoughts. This thinking, which is descriptively unconscious, leads to resistance to the analysis of thoughts and becomes a crucial component of whether self-analysis is possible. At these times the patient may be accepting of the therapist seeing meaning in his or her thoughts, but the patient remains descriptively resistant to engaging in this aspect of the analytic work for him- or herself. Unless one keeps the patient's capacity for self-observation as an active component of the free-association method, an important impediment to self-analysis may not be analyzed. A patient's acceptance of the therapist's interpretation of meaning is a limited method of judging analytic change.

Increasing understanding of the role of the ego in the psychoanalytic process allows us to understand the changes in the patient's orientation in relationship to his or her thoughts, as aspects of conflict are brought into awareness. While data from follow-up studies indicate the importance of the development of self-analysis, Loewald (1971, 1975) suggests that what one sees in successful analyses in areas of conflict is the move from lower- to higher-level ego functioning. Descriptively, we see this in the way patients can move from total immersion in the affective truth of a transference reaction, to the capacity to step back from it momentarily and wonder why they might be feeling the way they are. One sees a movement from thinking based upon what Piaget (Inhelder and Piaget 1958) called "preoperational" thought to that based more on "formal" operations. Developmentally, it is only in adolescence that the capacity for thinking back on one's thoughts using a variety of perspectives is possible. Thus, a patient under the influence of preoperational thought does not look for ambiguities, contradictions, or irrationality in his or her thoughts. As Flavell (1963) notes, the person thinks but cannot think about his or her thinking (p. 156).

Thus, in the early stages of treatment one would not expect reflective thought in areas of conflict. The ego in a regressive state is not capable of looking back on itself, while in nonconflictual areas self-reflection may be highly developed. As more components of the conflicts are brought into awareness, there is a move from actions and thoughts being closely intertwined—as they are in preoperational thought (see Busch 1989 and Chapter 6, this volume)—to the capacity for objectifying thoughts and reflecting back on them. Thought now shows a greater flexibility, with the capacity to turn back on itself to examine all that is there.

From this perspective, movement toward increasing self-observation is a developmental step in thinking that then enhances the self-analytic process. Self-analysis without self-observation seems a contradiction in terms. How conscious this process needs to be, however, is not yet clear. Seeing the capacity to reflect as a developmental step in the analytic process, then, changes the view of the free-association method. Observing one's thoughts as they are occurring is one developmental step; being able to then think about what one is thinking is still another developmental step.

In contrast to Freud's initial view of reflection and observation, we now see it as a vital capacity for continuing self-analysis. Without the ability to observe thoughts along with the resistances to thoughts in action, it is difficult to see how a patient may find meaning in them. It is, after all, a major analytic accomplishment when a patient recognizes that there is something in his or her thoughts or actions to understand and that it can be helpful to understand. This whole process can be seen most dramatically with patients whom we see in a second analysis. These patients will frequently show the capacity for reflective observation, except in areas of unanalyzed conflict in which they remain blind to the possibility that there is something to be observed.

CONCLUDING THOUGHTS

For a variety of historic reasons, our method of instructing patients in free association as first explicated by Freud is designed to circumvent resistances and keep the *therapist's* ability to understand the associations at the forefront of analytic technique. This is not surprising, as Freud's views on the method of free association were developed at a time when his understanding of the psychoanalytic task was very different from our current views. Furthermore, "Freud repeated himself on this important topic, and though he came back to it again and again throughout his life, he never got far beyond some early core ideas" (Mahoney 1979, p. 163). Based on a particular patient population, which contributed to a theory of anxiety and the unconscious heavily influenced by nineteenth-century views of energic principles, Freud's view of cure was the verbalization of unconscious ideation. Furthermore, his great discovery of meaning behind seemingly random thoughts and actions ultimately led to a view of the therapist's role as a type of psychic cryptographer. In conjunction, these two perspectives led to the model of the patient as a provider of primary data on his or her unconscious fantasy life, while the therapist became the reader of these data. As has been pointed out, Freud never fully integrated his ego psychology with technique (Busch 1992,

1993, Gray 1982). Furthermore, later forays into ego psychology tended toward understanding normal development, not the role of the ego in the clinical process. This has hampered our understanding of the ego in the psychoanalytic process as exemplified in our uncritical (for the most part) acceptance of the method of free association as first described by Freud.

It seems clear that therapists need to reorient themselves to the method of free association. This process would include taking into account Freud's second theory of anxiety and the growing body of data on what is essentially psychoanalytic in the psychoanalytic process (i.e., follow-up studies showing the significance of self-analysis in successful analyses). Whereas Freud's first theory of anxiety explains symptom formation as being due to dammed-up libido, his second theory emphasizes danger to the ego as the basis of the sense of threat. What is significant is that Freud's second theory of anxiety seems only to have been episodically grasped in our written history (see Chapter 5). A therapist's orientation toward resistances to free associations will differ dramatically based on his or her stance vis-à-vis the source of anxiety.

One important component of the lag in evaluating the method of free association is the tension that exists between psychoanalysis as the understanding of meaning in memory and psychoanalysis as the understanding of meaning in process. Thus, considerable disagreement exists on the appropriate stance of the therapist when listening to a patient's masturbatory fantasy told with a great many pauses. The psychoanalytic stance from the position of memory is to try and understand the meaning of the fantasy in the context of the general transferential ambience as a repetition of the past. The psychoanalytic process stance would highlight the meaning of the pauses, especially within the understanding of ongoing, demonstrable ego resistances. Psychoanalysis, from its very beginning, has been the study of memory. While Freud was well aware of the clinical importance of the psychoanalytic process, this understanding became lost in the ill-fated theoretical link among repetitions in action, the repetition compulsion, and the death instinct. Traditionally, the patient has been viewed as the purveyor of associations. We have been much slower to integrate the associative *process* into our work, especially the ego's role in it as seen in surface manifestations of conflict.

Differences currently exist in how the free associations are viewed among not only obviously divergent schools but also those that might be considered similar in persuasion. Thus, there are subtle but important differences in the nature of what the therapist is looking for, as seen in in the work of Arlow and Brenner (1990) and Gray (1992).

> In doing so [demonstrating transference], the analyst helps the patient to distinguish between fantasy and reality, between past and present. It becomes possible to demonstrate to the patient how much his or her thought and behavior are determined by unconscious conflicts and fantasies deriving from the past. [Arlow and Brenner pp. 681–682]

> My aim is a consistent approach to *all* of the patient's words, with priority given to what is going on with and within those productions as they make their appearance, not with attempts to theorize about what was in mind at some other time and place. [Gray p. 324]

Protestations aside about the many similarities in outlook between these therapists, there is a subtle but significant difference between them in their view of the associative process. Arlow and Brenner are geared more toward the elucidation of the *meaning* of the associations and their echoes from the past, while Gray is focused more on the immediate conflict as seen in the *process* of associating. This difference in emphasis reflects continuing tensions between unintegrated components of the topographic model, especially the role of consciousness, that linger in limbo in the structural model. Thus, while few therapists would disagree with the importance of elucidating unconscious fantasies, it remains cloudy as to how this is best accomplished in the face of ongoing unconscious resistances, which themselves may become the repository of wishes that are then defended against. Proponents champion one side of the conflict and tend to finesse this issue. I believe this is one factor why Freud's view of the method of free association has not been sharply contrasted with an approach consistent with his later views on the resistances. That is, we blend these two approaches as we attempt to accommodate clinically to a thorny technical problem. Landau (in press) suggests the concepts ego syntonicity and dystonicity are more at the core of the structural theory than consciousness. This promising line of thought orients the psychoanalytic clinician to the patient's associations from the perspective of the ego, a perspective that has been missing in our conceptual understanding of the method of free association. It orients the clinician to the ego in the defense–drive oscillation typical in associations, while providing a new dimension for examining patients' views of their own thoughts.

In essence, then, this chapter is not so much about the words the therapist uses to describe the method of free association to patients (although I do not consider the words insignificant) but about the orientation of the two participants toward the process. Our heritage has been geared toward using the method to bypass the ego's participation. Taking advantage of our increased understanding of the role of the ego as mediator of psychic threat, as well as the seat of the observation of conflict, we could most fruitfully turn (again) analytic interest in the patient's free associations toward the ego. Primary use of other orientations to the process of free association has the potential for colluding with the wish to avoid threat by circumventing the resistances and meeting certain regressive gratifications.

BEGINNING
A TREATMENT

One of Freud's (1913) most cited similes is his likening psychoanalysis to chess, in which only the beginning and ending moves are open to a definite plan, while the middle defies any such delineation. History has shown him to be correct about the middle phase, while the beginning has proven equally unyielding to prescriptive portrayals. While Freud's clinical predilictions led him to understand that beginning a psychoanalysis had to do with the patient's introduction to a unique *process* (i.e., the method of free association), his prestructural theory led him to focus on the therapist's tasks at the expense of the patient's. The limited literature on this topic seems to have maintained this tilt toward what the *therapist* needs to do in beginning an analysis. It is the contention of this chapter that a model of psychoanalysis, based upon the method of free association, is a useful one from the beginning for most patients. It is primarily through this method that what has increasingly become clear as the goals of an ego-psychological approach of the psychoanalytic method (i.e., increasing freedom of associations and self-analysis), are most effectively attainable.

Freud's (1913) seminal article on beginning an analysis is launched with some practical ground rules. These include advice on such things as reasons one avoids extensive discussions with patients before the analysis, how to deal with questions about the length of the analysis, and issues of appointment times and money. While the issues he raises are significant ones for any analysis and were especially significant at the time, since there were no other written guidelines for beginning an analysis, one gets the impression today of his suggestions being like introducing someone to the sport of basketball by describing the size of the court, the height of the basket, and the number of players on each side, while leaving out the intracies of team play and shooting and dribbling the ball for the ultimate purpose of putting the ball in the basket to score points.

In the second half of the article, Freud elaborates the technique of beginning an analysis and the reasons for it. While introducing the significance of the method of free association for a psychoanalysis to take place, Freud's instructions to the patient make it clear that he saw the necessity of overcoming the resistances based upon the topographic model and its emphasis primarily on making the unconscious conscious (Busch 1994). He consistently makes a familiar error (Busch 1992; Gray 1982) of seeing that one must take into acount the resistances when dealing with unconscious wishes, *but he does not yet see the necessity of taking similar precautions with the resistances*. Of course, it was not until the introduction of the structural theory that Freud recognized resistances as unconscious, and saw them as the result of a threat to the ego. However, even at this point the method of free association was used more to overcome than understand resistances.

Freud's (1913) view of the beginning of treatment can be summarized in the following manner. One begins by introducing the method of free association, which included exhortations to overcome the resistances.

> You will be tempted to say to yourself that this or that is
> irrelevant here, or is quite unimportant, or nonsensical, so
> that there is no need to say it. You must never give in to
> these criticisms, but must say it in spite of them—indeed,
> you must say it precisely *because* you feel an aversion to
> doing so. [p. 135]

One then waits for the positive transference to become established by showing sincere interest in what the patient is
saying and avoiding mistakes. Then, when the positive transference is established, it is used to overcome resistances. It is
only psychoanalysis "if the intensity of the transference has
been utilized for the overcoming of resistances" (p. 143).
Thus, Freud's view of the opening phase focuses on the
establishment of an analytic *process*, based upon the method
of free association. However, the topographic theory limited
his view of this process and how it might best be used,
emphasizing a compliant patient and authoritative analyst.
This model still exerts a subtle influence on technique, while
we have drifted away from the significance of the establishment of an analytic process in the opening phase.

A significant attempt to correct the paucity of literature
on beginning an analysis can be found in Jacobs and Rothstein's (1990) book on this topic. Their focus, brilliantly
achieved, is the opening phase from the perspective of unique
issues the therapist might be faced with in a variety of clinical
situations. This is captured in the titles of the chapters
(actually separately authored articles): "On Beginning an
Analysis with a Young Adult," "On Beginning a Reanalysis,"
"On Beginning with Candidates," "On Beginning with a
Reluctant Patient," "On Beginning with a Borderline Patient," "On Beginning with Patients Who Require Medica-
tion," and so forth. While a useful collection, chock-full of
insights, taken as a whole the book discarded Freud's notion
that there is an underlying psychoanalytic process that is
necessary to establish from the beginning of the analysis. It is
a continuation of a perspective, initially stated by Glover
(1955), that the opening phase of analysis is "determined less

by the conditions of analysis than by the spontaneous reactions of the patient" (p. 19). Beginning a psychoanalytic process has been exchanged for the more ambiguous model of establishing an atmosphere, *via understanding*, in which analysis can take place. Thus, in describing the stance of the "modern analyst" toward the beginning phase, Jacobs (1990) states:

> For what he has come to understand is that technique cannot be made rigid or formalized in rules but must be adaptable and responsive to the needs of the patient. This is particularly so in the opening phase when the analyst's capacity to grasp and respond to the communications and metacommunications being transmitted between himself and the patient is so critical a factor in the establishment of the kind of rapport that fosters the unfolding of an analytic process. [p. xv]

One cannot disagree with Jacobs's eschewing of bad technique for better atmosphere. However, his assumption seems to be that by paying attention to the technique of beginning an analysis, the therapist will be led astray from good atmosphere. I would maintain that understanding, without a demonstration of its contextual framework within the analytic process, is not necessarily helpful. It can encourage a regressive atmosphere while doing little to aid the patient in understanding how the use of the analytic process will be helpful. We have tended to focus on the analytic atmosphere and the therapist's understanding as the primary energizer of the process, while tending to underestimate the importance of the patient's understanding and use of the process—a point I shall return to many times. Jacob's view of what therapists have been traditionally taught as proper technique in the beginning phase—"analyzing from the surface downward, interpretation of fluid defenses before those embedded in character, and interpretation of affects before content" (p. xv)— has proven to be inconsistently applied and misunderstood (Apfelbaum and Gill 1989, Busch 1992, Gray 1982). Until recently, ego analysis has not been a

particularly strong suit in our psychoanalytic armamentarium of techniques. Brenner's (1990) suggestions for beginning an analysis suffers from similar problems.

> [T]he analyst's role is to be analytic, nothing more. An
> analyst tries to understand the motives for a patient's
> thoughts and behavior, the nature and origin of the pa-
> tient's conflicts, and to communicate that understanding
> to the patient in the best way at the best time (i.e., to offer
> correct and timely interpretations). That's what an analyst
> should do, or try to do, from the first to the last day of every
> analysis. [p. 55]

In one sense, it is an unassailable position. Who could
argue against the importance of the therapist's understanding for the success of the analysis? Yet this perspective
ignores the differences among therapists over what it means
to be analytic. Furthermore, what we consider to be correct
and timely has been infrequently articulated, is often subtly
effected by prestructural notions (Busch 1992, 1993, 1994),
and overlooks the ego's detailed role in initiating resistances
as part of the compromise formations. Most importantly,
Brenner's position subtly moves the frame of the opening
phase to the therapist and his or her understanding and away
from the establishment of an analytic process. This has
significant consequences for how the opening phase of analysis is conducted, while also influencing the goals and purpose of an analysis. It is a demonstration of Gray's (1982)
astute observation of the distinction, among therapists, of
their *forms of attention* during analysis.

There is a framework, using the process of analysis,
within which most analyses take place, no matter what the
theoretical orientation of the therapist. The process is the
method of free association. As Kris (1990b) states, "[F]ree
association is the hallmark of psychoanalytic treatment conducted by analysts of every stripe" (p. 26). The framework
therapists all use is that patient's free associations are the
basic raw data of the analysis. Thus while there are differ-

ences among therapists in what they understand from the patient's associations, the basic frame across all therapists remains that the *patient's free associations are the primary data upon which the two particpants base their understanding.* It is my contention that from the beginning of analysis it is necessary to establish an analytic frame, that clearly delineates what the data of analysis will be. Like any frame, this becomes a necessity for giving shape and structure to the analysis. The structure I believe is necessary to establish is that it is the patient's free associations we will be analyzing, for the purpose of increasing freedom of thought and the capacity to see these thoughts as psychologically meaningful. While an empathic attunement or an appreciation of developmental concerns, to name just two factors, plays an important role in the patient's feeling understood and in the possible internalization of more benign introjects, there can be no self-analysis without the data of analysis being clear. If the patient does not know that what is being analyzed are his or her thoughts, the purpose of the analysis can become quite muddied. Furthermore, establishing the frame of the analytic process as described earlier tends to make interpretations more grounded and less reliant on an omniscient therapist who intensifies the patient's regressive transference and puts the patient in a passive position in relationship to understanding his or her own fantasy life. As Searl (1936) states, "[T]hat which is important is not the extent to which *we* may be able to impart to the patient our knowledge of his life and psyche, but it is the extent to which we can clear the patient's own way to it and give him freedom of access to his own mind" (p. 487).

It is surprising to see how, in many second analyses, patients have little idea of what the data of analysis are. Speculation, only tangentially related to their thoughts, seems a primary method of theory building. This is more understandable when one frequently hears colleagues interpreting in a similar manner. That is, the data that have led to the therapist's conclusions are too infrequently articulated. For example, in noticing that a patient turns away after expressing angry thoughts, the therapist might say, "Do you feel like looks could kill?" or "I noticed that right after you expressed your anger you turned away from me. I wonder if this is an indication that you are afraid that looking at me, when you're angry, could be dangerous?" A dilemma in intepretive strategies, as reflected in these two approaches, has been part of a tension in psychoanalytic technique since its beginning (Apfelbaum and Gill 1989, Busch 1992, 1993, 1994, 1995d, Gray 1982).

As I have pointed out elsewhere (see Chapter 6), a patient's thought processes throughout much of an analysis, but especially in the opening phase, are very concrete. This is due to certain qualities of cognition that remain through early latency, resulting in thinking about conflicts that never advance much beyond a concrete stage (Sandler 1975) or that remain as regressive flashpoints. The same is true of the capacity to reflect back on thoughts as a stable component of one's core cognitive processes. Within this context, the analytic frame I have described— using the patient's free associations as the basic data of analysis— serves as an ideal method for analyzing thinking that is concrete and nonreflective. Put most succinctly, it concretizes the analytic task at a time when the patient's thinking is most concrete. When looked at in its essentials, the analytic process can be conceived as following what the patient is allowing into his or her mind, what is allowed to be connected with what, when there are interferences with this, and what the patient is doing with his or her thoughts while talking (i.e., thoughts as gifts , questions, demands, etc.). This becomes a different view of the process than the therapist's as interpreter of "absent content" (Searl 1936), in which the primary function of the analysis becomes the therapist's search for meaning in the figure of the patient's ground. Such methods are not as congruent with a patients's cognitive capacities, especially in the beginning of an analysis. For the patient, feeling that the therapist is in empathic attunement may be an important component of the initial phase of the analysis, but knowing how the therapist got to that point in a concrete manner does much to cement the importance of the process to the future of the analytic work.

What psychoanalysis has to offer, in contrast to other forms of treatment, is self-analysis. Its cornerstone is the ability to allow thoughts to come to mind, while using these thoughts as the data that can be reflected back on to see whatever potential it might have for self-understanding. This deceptively modest goal requires the establishment of a framework for processing thoughts, a process that can and needs to begin in the opening phase. The danger, as Searl (1936) points out, is that

> [w]e are taking away the patient's accepted and reasonable responsibility if we in any way shift the importance away from the only, though very difficult, technique which analysis asks of him; and we encourage belief in magic, which is independent of conditions, if we do not evince our belief in the conditions in which analysis can be carried on. [p. 489]

CASE MATERIAL

In the first case, the reader will see what I am striving for in setting the analytic frame. It is not new or unique. It is one aspect of what has always been part of the "talking cure." However, the specifics of the method, and especially its importance for the opening phase, have not been emphasized enough. Essentially, what I am trying to convey to the patient is the notion that "if we listen carefully to your associations in a variety of ways, we can learn about the conflicts that brought you into the analysis." I try to stay closely tied to the patient's associations and bring them back in as the basis for my interpretation. Wherever possible, the method is less investigative, based less on questioning the patient, and based less on interpretation using "special" knowledge of dynamics or development.

Case 1

In his first analytic session, Dr. A. began with the realization that during the consultation, he forgot to tell me of a week-long convention he had registered for several months prior to our initial meeting that was to begin in one month's time. At this point he wasn't sure whether he would go. Although his wife wanted to go, he was uneasy about leaving because of a recent bout of acting out by his adolescent daughter. He thought they should stay home to prevent her from doing something self-destructive. He then recalled a time in college when he felt like he was out of control and no one seemed to notice. Mostly he described some drinking incidents that led to reckless driving. He also alluded to his impregnating his future wife, which led to their having to get married and the birth of the daughter. Yet, when he was younger, there were times when his parents did try to put controls on him and he resented it. I pointed out that he had come in talking about whether to go to the convention. This was then followed by his sense that he should be home to stop his daughter from doing something harmful, which reminded him of how he had no one to help him with his potentially harmful behavior. I told him that it seemed he was saying there was a part of him that might wish I would stop him from going to the convention. To not have controls put on him is to feel uncared for. Yet his dilemma is that he then resents these same controls he desires. Dr. A. noted this was a familiar feeling, but one he had not seen so clearly before. He then described how glad he was to get going in the analysis. It was clear to him that a lot was getting stirred up. Yet he was surprised at how easily he was talking about things.

Dr. A. began the second session by commenting on how he was aware of feeling more anxious. He then went on to describe a number of experiences in which he was unable to let his feelings emerge and he stayed in control. There was a recent ski trip when he and some friends, while in a small plane, were caught in a violent storm. He showed no feelings and was barely aware of any. As an adolescent, he went with some friends to a prostitute but was unable to get an erection. He still has this problem intermittently in sex with his wife, but overall felt they had a pretty good relationship. Now that they are both starting treatment, he worried what this would do to their relationship. His mother-in-law had been married numerous times, and so had both his brothers. His next older brother had been a terrible tease when they were growing up, and he use to get very mad at him. He then described a hunting trip he went on with his father and this same brother when they were in their teens. Dr. A. heard some rustling in the tall grass, saw some movement, and then saw a bird take flight. He wheeled and shot at the bird, and immediately he was striken by a feeling of horror at the possibility he had not shot high enough and might have hit someone kneeling in the grass where, of course, he had last seen his brother. His brother was not hurt, but the experience was still a vivid one that scared him.

I reminded him of how he started the session describing situations in which he kept his emotions in check. After talking about his worries over his anger toward his brother and the effect analysis might have on his marital relationship he told of fearing that, while acting spontaneously on the hunting trip, he was afraid he shot his brother. It suggested that his anxiety about coming in today had to do with his fear that the analysis would lessen his controls, leading him to hurt someone. I wondered whether one component of his question of the previous day (i.e., whether he should be "allowed" to go to the convention) was based on his feeling that he needed to be kept in check, or else he could be very dangerous. This led him to remember temper tantrums he had as a child, which was followed by a memory of a persistent childhood image of a desolute landscape with no other people. It was a depressing and scary memory. I suggested that in his thoughts we could see he was fearful that the emergence of his anger would leave him totally alone, and thus he felt the need to be kept in control. He then remembered how when he and his brother would squabble, his mother would threaten to leave and never come back if they didn't stop.

The remainder of the week, the theme was similar. The next session, after talking about sexual feelings he had toward a patient, he went on to describe his medical specialty as being like a time bomb waiting to go off as no data were available on long-term results. He limited his practice to a very small area so that he would not be in competition with other doctors. He ended with the concern that he was trying to go too fast in the analysis and needed to be slowed down. This was the major theme throughout the analysis—that is, Dr.A.'s feeling that he needed to be slowed down, or else his destructive sexual and aggressive feelings would emerge and he would be left alone. On the other hand, if he felt that others were attempting to place limits on him, he would become irritated. The result was that he lived a semi-reclusive life in which much of the decision making in his private life, and in his practice, was left to his wife. His medical specialty was one in which caution and control were at a premium.

I have tried to indicate how I establish an analytic frame from the beginning of treatment. By staying closely tied to what the patient is saying, I try to convey that analysis is a process of listening to one's thoughts. The content, form, and sequencing of thoughts become the primary basis of forming interpretations of the patient's conflicts. Within this framework, I hope to convey that the data are there for understanding but it needs to be listened to.[1] A primary factor that emerges, of course, is that there are dangers associated with the act of listening to oneself, which are a mirror of the conflicts that brought the patient to the analysis. As important, though, is my assumption that during the opening phase we will be dealing with a patient who, in areas of conflict, will be concrete in thought and show a limited ability for self-reflection. Gearing one's interpretations to this type of

---

1. Another therapist might put together the associations in a different form. The reasons for this go far beyond the scope of this study. All I am trying to convey is the importance for the development of an analytic process on focusing on the data of analysis (i.e., free associations) from the beginning.

thinking in a way that is useful and meaningful for the patient is a constant strain on the therapist's capacity to integrate various levels of communication in the patient's thoughts, while reflecting back to the patient in a usable, concrete fashion connected to what he or she can be conscious of in his or her thoughts. If done well, the patient is impressed more with what is on his or her mind than with the therapist's ability to read or understand what is on the patient's mind.

Case 2

Mr. B., a lawyer, had been in psychotherapy for about one year because of feelings that he was unable to reach his potential. After a summer vacation this was his first analytic session with a candidate in psychoanalytic training. He started out by saying that he would probably fall asleep. He was back at work and had had an anxiety attack the previous night. He got a call from a woman with whom he had a brief affair early in his marriage. She wanted to know whether he was going to an upcoming meeting, with hints that she would be available for a fling. He said he didn't think it would be a good idea. He then started talking of a woman in his firm whom the partners had decided to let go. She was very bright but terribly neurotic, and they decided they had to do what was best for the firm. He was speaking to a friend at another firm recently, and he was told of how they were hiring someone who they knew would not work out but they needed another body to do the work. "They don't give a shit he'll piss away a year of his life." He then remembered that his insurance form for the therapy was sent to the office manager, and she asked him about it. He was upset that someone would know about this. He didn't know how comfortable he would be going into the office late on Wednesdays. "Then I thought of coming in today," he said, "and I got anxious." The candidate then said, "So there is anxiety, discomfort, about starting." Mr. B. agreed but also was concerned about his loss of privacy and people at work finding out about his being in psychoanalysis. Therapy is one thing, but analysis is something else. He then started talking about the possibility of taking a fellowship in Washington, D.C., for a year.

While the candidate picked up on what I would also see as a significant affect that needed to be addressed (i.e., anxiety), he did so in a manner that requires the patient to accept his view as an authority, while missing an opportunity to begin to show him how his use of the method of free association can help understand his feelings. He comes in describing himself as anxious the previous evening, and then associates to a secret affair. His experienced anxiety later in the session is again associated with a clandestine relationship (i.e., analysis). He further elaborates on this when he expresses concern over the use of the couch, which he sees as placing him in a passive position (i.e., falling asleep). In the background, also, are feelings associated with someone being dumped after a year (the time he was in psychotherapy before the vacation and the beginning of the analysis), which suggests defended-against feelings about his absence from the therapist. How I would pick up on these various associations depends on where the patient had gotten to in his therapy to this point. At the very least I would suggest that his anxiety over beginning the analysis had to do with his fear that he would become more passive and that it was like starting a clandestine relationship that would not be good for him.The anxiety over his association of passivity with becoming a woman, and the fears associated with longings stirred up by the vacation could be brought in depending on the work that had been done to that point.

In the second session, the patient started out talking about how chaotic it was getting to analysis in the early morning when he had to get his daughter ready for school. He didn't know how he was going to do this. He then wondered briefly whether in a previous treatment he had ever used the couch, and then talked of his passivity in waiting to see whether certain job offers come in. He felt he wasn't used to being so passive. His thoughts then turned to a great ruling he had obtained for a client that he felt was unappreciated by the other lawyers in his firm. His daughter was wonderful (i.e., perfectly quiet) when examined by her pediatrician. This led him to complain about his law practice. He wanted to be a lawyer, not a businessman. Everything was so competitive in this town. Some people were wildly competitive, while he felt he only had competed with himself. He went on to describe various triumphs after which there was some misfortune. He was valedictorian of his class, but he got sick and missed graduation. It didn't really matter since he wanted to be on the football team, not the one with the best grades. When he got into a prestigious university, it was a bigger deal to others than to him. He ended the session complaining that his parents never said much to him.[2]

In this session, there are mounting concerns about the feelings stirred up, with the patient feeling uncomfortable enough that thoughts of stopping are in the background, as they were in the first session. Again I would reiterate his connection between being on the couch and feeling heightened passivity. I might note that feeling unappreciated leads to thoughts of someone (his daughter) who was appreciated for her passivity and then point out how he associates this with being "good," like a girl. Finally, he gives various examples in which success is followed by misfortune (valedictorian then illness), a minimizing of his success (he didn't want to be valedictorian anyway or get into a prestigious university), and a seeming lack of interest in competition with others (he just competes with himself). His fears about being in analysis seem a result of his view that he will have to become passive (like his view of what it means to be a woman). While on the one hand this attitude seems to be making beginning analysis increasingly uncomfortable, it is a position he seems to feel is necessary in order to be appreciated. Furthermore, he links it with a dificulty in

---

2. This seems to be a reference to the therapist's silence, which is intensifying the conflicts to be described. Since I would probably be saying more to the patient, I will not attempt to integrate this association with what I would say.

feeling good about his successes and being competitive. It seems possible that his feelings about competing with others are affected by his concern that one cannot do this and remain valued.

As in the first case, I would be striving to make my interventions as concrete and experience-near to the patient's associations as possible. Again, this not only matches a way of thinking characteristic of patients in the midst of conflict but also is a beginning of the process. We are trying to convey that by listening carefully to the patient's thoughts, we will be able to understand his or her conflicts in an immediate way, which will be a reflection of those issues that brought the person into treatment in the first place. Thus, in both cases we can demonstrate that associations are directly linked to central, core conflicts, while establishing the basis of self-analysis. To paraphrase Gray (1973), when this different way of perceiving thoughts is taken for granted by the therapist and left unarticulated, the resulting interpretations may fail to take into account how fully the psychic conflict can be observed via the patient's associations. "When this is the case, how can the patient come to gain a maximum grasp of this part of his own self-observing capacities?" (p. 475).

Inevitably, the use of free association becomes part of a transference repetition. Thus, the associations themselves become a gift to the therapist, a part of a sadomasochistic battle, a way to keep thoughts in control—the varieties are endless. It facilitates highlighting what a patient is doing with his or her thoughts when the method of free association is firmly established as a basis for analytic understanding.

CONCLUDING THOUGHTS

Stone's (1954, 1961) perceptive remarks on the analytic situation presaged many changes in psychoanalysis. For example, one can see a direct link between Jacobs's (1990) emphasis on the importance of the analytic atmosphere and comments made by Stone some thirty years earlier.

> However, I must state my conviction that a nuance of the analyst's attitude can determine the difference between a lonely vacuum and a controlled but warm situation. . . . The rigors of the analytic situation are subtle and cumulative, importantly operative, *whether evident or not.* It is one of the burdens of this presentation to suggest that the intrinsic formal stringencies of the situation are sufficient to contraindicate superfluous deprivations in the analyst's personal attitude. [1961, pp. 21–22]

However, Stone points to another component of the therapist's stance that still lingers, what he calls the "patient-as-cadaver" paradigm. The prototypical model "preserved intact, indeed in some respects exaggeratedly, the traditional features of the physician–patient personal relationship: ostensibly omniscient, authoritarian, helpful on one side; ignorant, utterly submissive, requiring help, on the other" (p. 13).

What has not been so clear, though, is how this model serves as a silent archetype of current psychoanalytic practice as well. The method of free association as initially elaborated by Freud (1900) put the patient in the position of a conduit. The prototypical example is of a passenger on a train having a variety of thoughts drifting into his mind, with the added requirement that these should now be verbalized for the therapist. The patient was *admonished* to keep critical thoughts from interfering with this task, with the warning that the whole enterprise would become impossible if these exhortations were not acknowledged. Self-reflection was discouraged.

As noted in the previous chapter, this tone of analytic exhortation not only is a model from the past but subtly creeps into current methods of establishing the method of free association. Furthermore, the cornerstone of the initial phase, resistance analysis, remained an authoritarian, non-collaborative model throughout Freud's writings. What Freud called working through resistances was, in reality, an attempt via the positive transference to induce the patient to give up the resistances by influence, education, and force of argument. Again, this is a model not only from our distant past (Busch 1992, Gray 1982).

Jacobs and Rothstein's (1990) book on beginning an analysis conveys some of this same attitude. The emphasis is on what the *therapist* needs to be thinking about to aid in the process of, to paraphrase Brenner, the *therapist* being more analytic. The framework emphasized by Jacobs and Rothstein is that in order for the analysis to begin well, it is the *therapist* and his or her understanding that need to be upgraded. The patient's role is passive, being limited to being well understood. The notion of the need to articulate a process for the patient that will help make him or her a participant is secondary or absent. The model these authors are working on is the therapist as an expert who conveys understanding. It fits in with certain omnipotent and passive needs of patients to be understood, with little participation on their parts. Taken to an extreme, the psychotherapist becomes a type of psychological detective, looking for hidden motives, obscured fantasies, missing data, and the plethora of events Searl (1936) classifies under the inspired term, *absent content.* It is not that the therapist should not look for these types of data in an analysis, but as a primary technical stance, this model sets a tone antithetical to what seems to me to be one of the important goals of analysis—self-analysis and an understanding of the resistances to it.

The idealized epiphany of my own analytic education was when a senior analyst stunned an audience at a national meeting by correctly guessing an obscure fact about a patient from the clinical data, further reinforced by the reverence shown for Kris's (1956b) reconstruction of omissions and distortions that are frequently screened by a richly elaborated family history. In this model, the therapist and his or her knowledge are at the center of the analytic task. However, it was Searl (1936) who pointed out the problem with this model almost sixty years ago. "The dynamics of the patient's disability to find his own way have been comparatively untouched if the resistance was more than the thinnest of crusts, and will therefore still be at work to some extent and in some form whatever the change brought about by the interpretation of absent content (p. 479).

Abend's (1990) perspective serves as a useful contrast. In writing about beginning with patients with prior knowledge about analysis, he states,

> Helping the patient at the very start of analysis to become aware that he has ideas in his mind that he hardly knew were present, that these exert an influence on his behavior in sessions, and that uncovering these beliefs can help explain why he behaves as he does, is a useful introduction to what lies ahead. There is no one special technique recommended for bringing out the preexisting ideas about analysis. Merely by keeping in mind that patients probably possess theories and ideas about analysis, analysts will be more likely to take that possibility into account in formulating interventions during the opening phase of analysis, especially when the patients' idiosyncratic reactions to the analytic situation make their appearance. [p. 60]

While agreeing entirely with the substance of Abend's comments, I believe the focus in his remarks is on the therapist and what he or she needs to keep in mind in order to facilitate the process. Again it is the therapist and his or her understanding that are at center stage. It isn't that I find this perspective inaccurate; it simply tilts the psychoanalytic process in a particular manner that can undermine the process of including the patient in the analytic process. The technique of how one communicates material to the patient is of some importance. It will have as decisive an impact on the purpose, goals , and outcome of the analysis as whether we correctly identify unconscious fantasies. We have tended in our literature to focus on the latter, with less attention to the former.

Compare Jacobs and Rothstein's model to Gray's paradigm in which the goals of the analysis are defined in terms of the patient's conscious "and increasingly voluntary co-partnership with the analyst" (1982, p. 624) and in which the therapist's "aim is a consistent approach to all the patient's words, with priority given to what is going on with and within those productions as they make their appearance, not with attempts to theorize about what was in mind at some other time and place" (1992, p. 324). This returns us to a free association–based model like Kris's that closely monitors the patient's associations to demonstrate, among other purposes, one aspect or another of the conflicts expressed in that data. It is a method that attempts to take into account the role of the ego and its important monitoring and integrating functions. Although analysis touches people in many different ways, it is through the conscious ego that self-analysis is accomplished. By attempting to include the conscious ego in our interpretive strategies, we go a long way toward aiding the process of self-analysis (Busch 1993). This outcome is a factor in why it is important to work within the frame I have been discussing.

While many forms of treatment can offer understanding, what seems to be uniquely psychoanalytic is that a process takes place that allows for the potential for self-analysis. This quality seems to be the hallmark of successful analyses (Schlessinger and Robbins 1983), and it depends on the development of self-observational qualities. By utilizing and drawing attention to the process of analysis from the very beginning, we highlight its importance for self-understanding. Increasing attention has been paid to this issue. In describing the significance of the psychoanalytic process, Weinshel (1984) sees it as "remaining as permanent products of the reasonably successful analysis and that their presence is reflected most immediately and most tangentially in the operation of a more effective and 'objective' capacity for self observaton" (p. 82). Gray (1986) sees self-observation not so much as a by-product of analysis as its focus. "Systematic attention to self observation, when clinically appropriate, can become a more explicit aim of analysis of the neurosis'' (Gray 1986, p. 260).

How we as therapists conceptualize the opening phase has much to do with how we think analysis works. My own view, outlined earlier, is based on my conviction that we have not sufficiently mined the analytic technique of listening closely to the patient's associations in a way that is easily usable by the patient. Greater attention needs to be paid to the work of analysis as a demonstration of the work of analysis.

5

RESISTANCE ANALYSIS

While the analysis of resistances has been a cornerstone of modern psychoanalytic technique, our understanding of the concept remains somewhat confused. One hears it referred to far too rarely in clinical discussions, while published papers dealing with the topic most often fluctuate between its pre- and post-structural meanings and the technical implications inherent in these positions. As Schafer (1983) has stated, "Certain things about resisting which ought to be well known, and are said to be well known and sufficiently appreciated and applied, are in fact not known well enough and not consistently attended to in practice" (p. 66). Gray (1982) has charitably called this muddled understanding of one of our basic concepts a "developmental lag," while reminding us that our understanding of theory informs our clinical stance.

Although thinking of this lag as a thing of the past may be comforting, it would be erroneous to do so. Many therapists still eschew an ego-psychological approach to resistance analysis in favor of a prestructural method, with its primary emphasis on unearthing the derivatives of the unconscious fantasy. In the recent definition of resistances given by Moore and Fine (1990), both views are given as if they were part of an integrated perspective rather than alternate points of view. Thus, while presenting many ideas on the ego's contribution to the resistances similar to those in this chapter, the authors end their discussion with the following passage:

> Once the patient's unconscious conflicts have been uncovered and some insight obtained, resistances may lead to delay or even failure to progress, reflecting an unconsciously determined reluctance to give up inappropriate childhood wishes and their maladaptive, defensively distorted expressions in symptoms, character, or behavior. Moreover, the relief or mental equilibrium that the neurotic symptoms achieved for the individual is hard to give up. These many factors contributing to resistance make the process of working through an essential part of analytic work. [p. 169]

In this perspective, one sees a return to a drive-dominated view of the resistances. The role of the unconscious ego in the working-through process is underemphasized when compared to the fixated drives. The complexity of understanding and bringing into awareness the unconscious dangers perceived by the ego, as well as the adaptational component of the resistances, are downplayed in the working-through process. Delays in the patient's changing are primarily seen as sequels to the difficulty in giving up "inappropriate childhood wishes." This approach to the resistances seems to be an example of what Apfelbaum and Gill (1989) describe as a tendency on many therapists' part to see ego analysis as something one does prior to id analysis, rather than throughout an analysis. As we shall see later, the comparative role of the ego versus the drives in resistances was an issue Freud struggled with but never successfully resolved. In fact, the struggle is still going on.

Goldberger (1989), in a review of a book on resistances, comments on the pejorative tone that creeps into the discussions of resistances. This is a common phenomenon for those therapists who view resistances as primarily an impediment to id analysis. One author in this collection goes so far as to suggest that the concept of resistance analysis ought to be abandoned because of its potential harm to the analytic enterprise. Widely varying views of resistances still exist, and changes in technique based on an increased understanding of the ego have been difficult for many therapists to integrate into clinical technique. Furthermore, while some of the most useful recent insights into resistances have come from self psychology, Kohut's (1984) dismissiveness of ego psychology in general, and his misunderstanding of resistances in particular, have made integration of these insights into general psychoanalytical theory problematic at best. What Kohut describes as the narcissistic transferences can also be seen as resistances based upon the fear of ego disintegration (i.e., due to faulty mirroring, over- or understimulation, etc.). However, Kohut's view of what he calls traditional treatment is "an overcoming of resistances in order to make the unconscious conscious" (p. 111). From this one can see how errors in understanding, perpetuated through the years, can skew the utilization of clinical insight.

Freud recognized resistances early (Freud 1895), often came back to the topic (Freud 1913, 1914, 1917a,b, 1926, 1937a,b, 1940), and saw resistances as serving many purposes and being due to a number of causes (e.g., defensive and unconscious gratification, secondary gain, superego guilt, the repetition compulsion-adhesiveness of the libido, just to name a few). Here I will focus on the defense resistances (unconscious ego resistances). For the sake of simplicity, I will be referring to them only as "resistances." While I will be talking about their role in defense, it should be noted at the outset that I see resistances as complex acts with contributions from many sources. The most salient resistances are often found to serve purposes of defense, drive gratification, adaptation, and transference. However, it has been the defense aspect of the resistances that has been the most baffling for therapists to integrate consistently into clinical technique, so it is this component of the resistance I will highlight. I will focus on persistent problems in the interpretation of resistances in the hope that understanding subtle resistances to the interpretation of resistances embedded in our theory and technical approaches will serve as a useful adjunct to Gray's work on the technique of resistance interpretation. As with any investigation of persistent resistances, the hope is that expanded ego awareness will lead to greater conceptual freedom in our approach to the resistances.

The resistances I will be referring to are not only the most overt types, such as missed appointments or silences. My perspective is similar to that of other psychoanalytic authors (Glover 1955, Stone 1973) who believe anything can be used as a resistance. Thus one can find resistances in the way patients associate, or do not associate. Or the way they tell a dream, or keep bringing dreams, or do not tell dreams, or do not listen, or the way they listen—all can be potential resistances. A patient rushing through his thoughts may be expressing one kind of resistance, while a patient who needs to pause between every thought may be expressing another type. Anything that interferes with the patient's ability to look at what is coming to mind, how it is coming to mind, and why it is coming to mind may be expressing one form of a resistance.

HISTORIC ANTECEDENTS
OF CURRENT AMBIGUITIES

Differences between clinical techniques of resistance analysis are mainly based on how closely the analyst follows the view of "the ego as the sole seat of anxiety" (Freud 1926, p. 161, italics added) and in one's understanding of the differences between Freud's first and second theory of anxiety. "Whereas the old view made it natural to suppose that anxiety arose from the libido belonging to the repressed instinctual impulses, the new one, on the contrary, made the ego the source of anxiety" (Freud 1926, p. 161). It has not been clearly emphasized that it was only with the introduction of the structural theory and the second theory of anxiety that a full psychoanalytic meaning of working with resistances was possible. Before this, the anxiety leading to the resistance was seen as a by-product of dammed-up libido. Therefore, the primary purpose of the psychoanalytic clinician was to free the libido by bringing the unconscious libidinal wishes into consciousness. The resistances were a barrier to be overcome, although not in the old sense as in the hypnotic phase when the resistances were bypassed completely. Instead, after the resistances were brought into consciousness, the psychotherapist was called upon to use various methods (e.g., promises of rewards of health, positive transference, suggestion) to help the patient push on in the face of resistances.

In Freud's second theory of anxiety, the ego was now seen as the source of anxiety. That is, anxiety was seen to occur when the ego perceived a danger (i.e., where it feared being overwhelmed), which was further seen as a repetition of an earlier traumatic situation. The resistances were now seen as the ego's response to anxiety. With this conceptual understanding of the underlying psychic mechanisms in place, psychotherapists could then grasp the full meaning of the resistances as the result of a perceived danger to the ego. Thus, the importance of Freud's second theory of anxiety is that (1) for the first time resistances could be understood in a psychodynamic rather than an energic fashion and (2) a psychoanalytic working through of these resistances could truly be undertaken that would center on an understanding of the danger to the ego underlying the resistance.

What is striking is that the clinical implications of Freud's second theory of anxiety seem only to have been episodically grasped in our psychoanalytic history. Although Freud's clinical brilliance led him to understand that resistances were an inevitable, necessary, and even useful component of the psychoanalytic method, he never fully appreciated the clinical potential of working with resistances. Even after he realized that the source of anxiety was in the unconscious ego's response to a perceived threat, his clinical approach to the resistances was primarily guided by earlier views. In these works, Freud (1914, 1917a,b,c) described the necessity for "working through" resistances, but what he meant by this was using suggestion, influence, and interpretation from above in what we would today call attempts to overcome the resistance. This was a working through only in the sense that it did not bypass the resistances entirely. In those earlier papers (e.g., Freud, 1917a,b,c) in which Freud started to recognize the resistance as a response to danger, his interpretive mode remained one attempting to overcome the resistance. This technique was consistent with his first theory of anxiety. Even after his discovery of the source of resistance as the ego's experience of anxiety due to fears of being overwhelmed, his technical approach to the resistances as expressed in an addendum to "Inhibitions, Symptoms, and Anxiety" (Freud 1926) remained essentially unchanged.

> If the resistance is itself unconscious, as so often happens owing to its connection with the repressed material, we make it conscious. If it is conscious, or where it has become conscious, we bring forward logical arguments against it; we promise the ego rewards and advantages if it will give up its resistance. [p. 159]

Thus, in line with his understanding of the role of the unconscious ego in resistances, Freud recognized the importance of bringing the resistances to consciousness. However, once the resistances were conscious, he returned to his technical view of using influence or suggestion to enlist the ego's cooperation in dealing with these interferences. Even though Freud had opened the door to a purely psychological approach to the resistances (i.e., helping the patient understand the sources of anxiety and the danger behind this), it was left to others to explicate fully this point of view.

In an opinion I will elaborate later in this chapter, I suggest that Freud's tie to the economic model and the principles of energy underlying the psychic system made it difficult for him to see the full clinical significance of his brilliant discovery. Thus, while he emphasized the importance of purely psychical factors in the role of resistances, Freud's notions of working-through were still influenced by the concept of the energic powers of the repressed unconscious, which led to the view of the psychotherpist as a juggler working with metal objects in the face of a giant magnet. From this perspective, the therapist needed an equally powerful force (e.g., suggestion within the contect of a positive transference) to counteract the pull from the unconscious. This point of view was still evident when Freud returned to the topic of resistances in his later papers (1937a,b, 1940). With an appreciation for the difficulties in working through resistances bordering on pessimism, the threat to the ego as a major factor in these difficulties faded into the backround. Instead, contributions based upon economic principles (i.e., the death instinct, adhesiveness of the libido, and constitutional differences in the ego), which led to the ego's inability to modify the drives, were advanced (Freud 1937a). "Once again we are confronted with the importance of the quantitative factor, and once again we are reminded that analysis can only draw upon definite and limited amounts of energy which have to be measured against the hostile forces" (Freud 1937a, p. 240).

Freud's dual view of resistances as something to be overcome versus a psychical act that could be understood is one factor in our muddled understanding of resistances. As I will show, this same duality keeps appearing in our literature on the subject of resistances. There are those who grasped the psychoanalytic meanings of working with resistances inherent in Freud's second theory of anxiety. However, contemporaneously with these same authors, and seemingly not influenced by them, there exist others who reflect Freud's ambivalence toward a purely psychoanalytic understanding of the resistances. These authors present the psychoanalytic reader with the confusing task of integrating insights into the nature of resistances with technical suggestions that do not take into account the ego's response to a dangerous situation. What follows are highlights of the abovementioned trends in the literature that leave one with the impression of a concept in disarray.

Analytic writings on resistance, after Freud's presentation of the second theory of anxiety, started out in a most promising fashion. Reich (1933) was one of the first to grasp the significance of resistances in analytic work, and his ideas are echoed throughout the literature on the topic. Reich's work reflects his understanding of the resistances as the ego's response to danger, and he offers the first technical suggestions based on this premise that reflect truly psychoanalytical working through of the resistances and not simply overcoming them.

> The better way, then, is to approach first the defense of the ego which is more closely related to the conscious ego. One will tell the patient at first only that he is keeping silent because—"For one reason or another," that is, without touching upon the id-impulse—he is defending himself against the analysis, presumably because it has become somehow dangerous to him. [p. 65]

Thus, working on the premise of the resistance as a danger to the ego, Reich begins to elaborate on the procedure for analyzing the resistances. In current terminology he suggests the necessity of first identifying, and then clarifying the resistance, before the unconscious wishes can be interpreted. We recognize in this the beginnings of ego analysis, of which the analysis of the resistance is a major component. However, Reich is not consistent in applying this perspective. As Schafer (1983) notes:

> Reich himself shows in his militaristic metaphors of armor and attack how much one may fall into an adversarial view of the analytic relationship. Despite his rich understanding

of the analysand's needing to resist and the complex
meaning or function of this policy, he, like so many others,
lapses into speaking of it as though it were a motiveless
form of stubbornness or belligerence. [p. 73].

It is as if Reich approached the resistances *simultaneously*
from two different perspectives—as an ego under threat and
as a blockade that must be overcome. It is not the only time
we will come upon such an apparent paradox in our literature
review.

Three years after Reich's book, Searl (1936) added brilliantly to the beginning psychoanalytic understanding of
resistance. Searl accomplished two major tasks in this paper
that had not occurred before. She integrates and expands
Freud's views of the ego resistance into the clinical realm,
while also pointing to the problems that occur if ego analysis
does not take place. Searl approaches the resistances as
adaptive responses that attempt to manage frightening emotions. This stance leads her to suggest, as Reich did before
her, that once a resistance is recognized, it is not enough to
help the patient overcome it with educative measures. She
notes the importance of understanding the reasons for its
formation (i.e., fear leading to an adaptive response) and the
patient's difficulty in emerging from it. Thus, Searl suggests
that unless the patient becomes aware of the reasons for
feeling like he or she will be overwhelmed, along with becoming aware of the feelings themselves, these will remain
unconscious, and no educative measures will have any
lasting effect. She goes one step further than Reich in stating
that once the resistances have been pointed out and clarified,
the specific nature of the danger the patient fears and where
it comes from needs to be analyzed. Finally, Searl subtly
describes the hazards of bypassing the resistances to get to
unconscious derivatives the patient is unaware of. She
points out that by doing this we miss the opportunity to work
with and strengthen the conscious components of the ego—a
significant point returned to only recently in the literature
(Busch 1993, Gray 1986, 1987, 1990, 1994).

A. Freud's (1936) earliest work champions the investigation of the ego and highlights how moments of conflict at the conscious surface can be used to great effect in analyzing resistances (Pray 1994). This is the point elaborated by Gray, but it remained unnoticed as a significant advance in technique until he resurrected the concept. Two analysts writing contemporaneously (Fenichel 1941, Sterba 1940) serve as good examples of how divergent views on resistance analysis can be taken from Freud's writing. Quoting liberally from Freud, Sterba takes the position that a transference resistance is just that—a transference *used* for the purpose of resistance. The fact that the resistance might be a by-product of the anxiety raised by the transference seems generally ignored by Sterba. The patient's expression of the transference is viewed as a resistance to remembering. Sterba's technical handling of the resistance, then, is to tell the patient that he or she has to give up the transference before the analysis can continue (p. 370).

Fenichel (1941), on the other hand, sees the implication of Freud's view of resistance as the ego's response to anxiety. Throughout his compact monograph *Problems of Psychoanalytic Technique*, he reminds the reader of the need to understand the affect generating the resistance in the ego before attempting to investigate the id content. Fenichel highlights the importance of analyzing the resistances throughout the analysis, while presenting the reader with what has become an all too familiar cautionary note on our lagging technique in dealing with the resistance.

> One of the stimuli to the development of so-called "analytic ego psychology" was insight into the fact that resistance in the analysis is a real therapeutic agent in that pursuing the aim of analyzing resistance has as a prerequisite a thorough analytic investigation particularly of chronic attitudes of resistance anchored in an individual's character. Here again, the volume of the literature concerning the newly gained psychological insight is incomparably greater than the number of papers which seek to utilize

this insight to contribute to an improvement of psychoanalytic technique. [p. 106]

Little appeared specifically on the topic of resistances until works by Glover (1955) and Greenson (1967). Glover's work is noteworthy in that, like Reich, he highlights numerous subtle aspects of resistances (e.g., resistances can invade all aspects of psychoanalytic work), while ignoring their importance as a response to danger. Greenson's work is especially intriguing in that he alternately champions, within a single, unified discussion, two separate approaches toward the resistances. He does this not to highlight the differences but to offer an integrated view of resistances.

Stone's (1973) pithy article is worth noting because it returns once again to a view of resistances as multifaceted dynamic constructions erected to ward off potentially disruptive affects. Stone points to the role of the ego in avoiding painful feelings as central in resistances, but he adds some thoughts that have been implicit in the work of others. First, Stone believes that therapists need to pay attention to what he calls the *affirmative, functional* aspects of the resistances. In this he is highlighting what Searl also noted, that resistances are brought into being because they were adaptive at one time. Second, Stone highlights the *self-protective* nature of resistances. He points to what the ego experiences as potentially disruptive affects that are being warded off by the resistances.

In summary, seeds of ambiguity are inherent in Freud's views of resistances. Even after his development of the second theory of anxiety and the corresponding view of resistances as the ego's response to danger, Freud found it difficult to give up his economic, drive-dominated view of resistances and the technical implications of this perspective. Following Freud, the literature on resistances frequently reflects his ambivalence. We continually see a return to a drive-dominated view of the resistances, with diminished importance given to understanding the role of unconscious

ego responses to danger. Growth in our clinical understanding of resistance has been stunted by confusion over the
basic meanings of resistances, while clinical technique has
lagged similarly. As both Gray (1982) and Schafer (1983)
have intimated, there is something about the ego resistances
that leads psychotherapists to protest their understanding of
the concept while continuing to present the same conceptual
errors in their thinking.

RESISTANCES AND CLINICAL TECHNIQUE: THE DUAL PERSPECTIVE

Since clinical theory informs clinical technique, we would
expect our tangled perspective on resistances to be reflected
in confusion over the clinical handling of resistances. No-
where is this seen more clearly than in the work of Greenson
(1967), partly because of his willingness to generously offer
us a window into his clinical work. What one sees are
numerous examples that perpetuate Freud's dual view of
resistances. On the one hand Greenson expresses a perspective that clearly reflects the influence of Freud's second
theory of anxiety:

> Thus I have the impression that no matter what the
> original source of an activity may be, its resistance func-
> tion is always derived from the ego. The other psychic
> structures have to be understood as operating through the
> ego. The motive for defense and resistance always is to
> avoid pain. [p. 87]

Yet at the same time numerous statements are made, and
examples given, that reflect a tendency to bypass the ego and
not take into account the "pain" Greenson sees as crucial in
understanding the resistances. I will spend some time discussing this aspect of Greenson's work, since it so accurately
reflects the dual perspective of resistances that has had such
a profound influence on clinical technique. It will also give us

the opportunity to explore some general issues of technique in resistance analysis.

One of Greenson's (1967) basic edicts is that the nature of what the patient is resisting can be boiled down to *what painful feeling he or she is trying to avoid* (p. 107). While this perspective seems based on Freud's second theory of anxiety, it leads Greenson to a technique that circumvents resistance analysis. Thus, Greenson describes how frequently, despite the patient's resistance, the affect will be expressed in non-verbal form (i.e., blushing, hiding, crossing legs together, etc.). He states:

> In all these instances, I am trying to detect the non-verbal, bodily reactions that are taking place. They may offer us clues as to what particular painful affect the patient is struggling with. If I think I can detect the specific affect, I confront the patient with, "You seem to be embarrassed, or afraid, or sad." [p. 108]

Note that Greenson seems less interested in why the feeling is being avoided or why it is painful than he is in what the affect is. He is more intent on picking up on whether the patient is hiding, embarrassed, shy, sad, and so forth, rather than why the patient is not able to be aware of or bring attention to what he or she is feeling. In this way Greenson is bypassing the resistance rather than exploring it. If a patient is keeping a feeling from awareness, one possibility we need to take into consideration, from the side of the resistance, is that there is some threat associated with the feeling coming into awareness. Thus, if we determine that it is a resistance leading to a feeling being kept from awareness, it is the threat we would want to focus on and not the feeling itself in isolation from the threat. In modifying Greenson's approach, I would suggest saying, "You seem to be feeling sad, but there is something about becoming aware of this feeling that seems dangerous to you." Here the emphasis is on the threat from becoming aware of the feeling. This is more in line with the nature of what a resistance is. Bringing the affect to light,

without focusing on the danger associated with being aware
of the feeling, becomes a bypassing of the resistance. It is
because the feeling is painful, as Greenson notes, that leads
to its entrance into awareness being resisted. However, by
attempting to get the feeling into consciousness, Greenson is
bypassing analyzing what this pain is about which has led to
the feeling's being kept from awareness. Thus, while stating
that the question of resistances can be reduced to what
painful feelings are being avoided, Greenson's clinical approach is based upon what *feeling* is being avoided, with the
fact that it is painful as secondary. However, if this were
indeed the essence of resistance, it would be just because the
feelings were painful that would lead to their being resisted,
and this would need to be the focus of the therapist's attention. Thus, Greenson's interpretive approach, as noted here,
leaves out the painful part of the resistance.

The problems Greenson (1967) gets into with his approach can be seen in the following example:

> A physician in analysis with me for several years begins to
> speak medical jargon in the middle of an analytic hour. In
> stilted tones he reports that his wife developed a "painful
> protruding hemorrhoid" just prior to a mountain trip they
> were planning. He said the news caused him "unmixed
> displeasure" and he wondered whether the hemorrhoid
> could be "surgically excised" or whether they would have
> to postpone their holiday. I could sense the latent anger he
> was withholding and could not refrain from saying: "I
> think you really mean that your wife's hemorrhoids are
> giving you a pain in the ass." He replied angrily: "That's
> right, you son of a bitch, I wish they would cut it out of her,
> I can't stand these women and their swellings that interfere
> with my pleasures." This last detail, incidentally, referred
> to his mother's pregnancy which precipitated his infantile
> neurosis at the age of five. [p. 67]

By confronting the patient with his latent anger (i.e., the
supposed painful feeling he is avoiding), Greenson gives up
the opportunity to explore how aware the patient is of his use

of medical terminology, and his thoughts about its use. In short, Greenson does not begin to *explore* what at this time is the most obvious resistance. It is insufficient to answer that Greenson seems to feel he knows what the resistance is to. It is insufficient because one is still bypassing the resistance and the chance for ego analysis with an invitation to the patient to participate. Why this patient is fearful of his anger, except in generic terms, is not answerable in Greenson's approach. He is interested more in getting out the strangulated affect than understanding the reasons for its being kept in.

As Schafer (1983) notes:

> There are many moments in the course of an analysis when analysands seem to dangle unexpressed content before the analyst. These are moments when the analyst is tempted to say, for example, "You are angry," "You are excited," or "You are shamed." But if it is so obvious, why isn't the analysand simply saying so or showing unmistakably that it is so? To begin with, it is the hesitation, the obstructing, the resisting that counts. If the analyst bypasses this difficulty with a direct question or confrontation, the analysand is too likely to feel seduced, violated, or otherwise coerced by the analyst who has in fact, even if unwittingly, taken sides unemphatically. [p. 75]

If one holds that resistances can be boiled down to a painful feeling that is being avoided, it can lead to a superficial approach to the resistances. This is why it is important to keep in mind that, from the perspective of resistance as defense, it is a threat to the ego that leads to resistances. This threat may be experienced as a painful feeling, but it is not necessarily synonymous with it. Furthermore, looking for the painful feelings behind the resistance and finding some underlying painful feeling easily leads one to fall far short of where one needs to get in working through a resistance. For example, finding out that a patient's restricted associations are due to embarrassment over exhibitionistic wishes is not equal to the uncovering of the reason for the resistance even though the painful affect has been discovered. The affect is a route into an understanding of the threat to the ego but cannot be considered synonymous with it. Thus, identifying the immediate affect that is causing the patient to be inhibited as embarrassment is a step toward working through the resistance, but a full understanding requires an articulation of the threat as well as its reasons for being there.

Greenson believes that in looking for the unconscious determinant of resistance, we are searching out the unconscious drives and their derivatives in thought. As he states, "After the resistance is demonstrable and clear, we're ready to interpret the unconscious determinants. That means we try to uncover the hidden instinctual impulses, fantasies or memories which are responsible for the resistance" (p. 112). Again Greenson confuses the issue when he describes impulses as the source of the resistances. Impulses, fantasies, or memories in themselves do not cause the resistances. Rather, it is the potential threat to the ego that these present that is the source of the resistances. By focusing on looking for the unconscious fantasies, we are again prone to bypass the resistances rather than interpret them. Ultimately, we hope to come to the unconscious impulses and their derivatives that cause the threat to the ego. However, seeking them out as our goal, once the resistance has been demonstrated, is to miss that the ego is unconsciously reacting to some threat. By bringing the unconscious fantasy to awareness, we do not remove the threat. By keeping our attention on the role of the threat to the unconscious ego, we are forced to keep in mind the importance of the ego in determining the form of resistance and its reasons for existence. In this way, we will avoid the tendency to bypass the resistance to get to the "real" content.

One of the most important components of the resistance that Greenson leaves out is their *adaptive side*. That is, it is important to remember that resistances are an adaptation to a threat to the ego at an earlier time. Thus, the patient who is silent in the face of emerging sexual thoughts toward the therapist is not simply withholding, or derailing the process, or illustrating any of the other interpretations of hostility that may be a part of any resistance. From the side of the ego resistance, the patient is responding to what is unconsciously experienced as a threat to which silence appears as a solution mirroring an earlier adaptation such as repression or oppositionalism as a regressive defense possibly designed to get the parents angry and thus deflect the threatening sexual fantasies.

The importance of recognizing the adaptive component of resistances cannot be overestimated. Most obviously, by keeping it in mind the therapist can help understand still yet another factor in the evolution of what likely will be a symptom-related piece of behavior. Furthermore, understanding the adaptive side to the resistances allows for an easier acceptance of the behavior for both therapist and patient. It takes some of the accusatory/guilt components out of the interpretive process if it can be seen by both the patient and therapist as a repetition of an earlier adaptation to something frightening.

SOME CURRENT PERSPECTIVES

No one has explored the role of resistances in as much depth as Paul Gray. In his work, resistance analysis is at the center of the psychoanalytic process, with the crucial component being an unconscious threat to the ego. The work of analysis involves identifying the resistance and analyzing the threat, for the purpose of allowing thoughts greater access to consciousness. He has, more than any other therapist, taken Freud's second theory of anxiety and applied it to technique.

The author most frequently mentioned as aligned with Gray in an ego-psychological approach to resistances is Schafer (1983), and indeed there are many similarities when compared to views dominated by the release of unconscious fantasies. However, there are subtle differences in their views of the resistances that have yet to be explored. Schafer's approach is presented as an antidote to the critical view of resistances that creeps into discussions when the role of the ego is not appreciated. Yet the centrality of the threat to the ego in resistances is noted only in passing in his work. While Gray highlights the significance of identifying resistances in order to make them conscious, Schafer frets over the implied criticism in such an approach (p. 169). Schafer does not seem as concerned as Gray in keeping closely attuned to what the patient is consciously aware of in his interventions (pp. 171–172). How far the therapist can stray from the surface and still make effective resistance interpretations is also a point of dispute.

Apfelbaum and Gill (1989) also trumpet the ego-psychological approach to the resistances. Many of their perspectives on resistances are similar to Gray's and Schafer's. Issues in common include the importance of the therapist's neutrality (p. 1087), consideration for ego syntonicity in resistance interpretations (p. 1090), and the therapist not taking on an authoritarian role (p. 1094). However, what Apfelbaum and Gill focus on is the subtle relationship between defense and what is being defended against, with the goal of defense analysis being to clarify the relationship between them.

Again, some subtle differences with Gray's work appear. Gray's technique of resistance analysis is directed toward uncovering and highlighting resistances in a manner that allows for the patient's greater *conscious* participation. His focus is more on the nature of the threat than the feelings or fantasies causing the threat. Gray's (1987) view is that the primary threat to the ego is from a superego, reexternalized onto the therapist, which was experienced first from an earlier authority figure. This is in contrast to Apfelbaum and Gill's (1989) view "that what is defense at one moment in relationship to a given wish may in the next moment become the wish defended against." (p. 1076). In their view, the distinction between the resistance and what is being resisted would only be a momentary one, with no primary threat easily established.

What seems most significant in these current works on

resistances is that the implications of Freud's second theory of anxiety are being explored, and some important questions on the nature of the ego and its consequences for clinical technique are being raised. For example, Gray's (1990a) method of listening for "breaks" in the associative process (p. 1087) to determine the moment of a resistance makes an assumption about the nature of ego functioning that is different from that of Schafer or Apfelbaum and Gill. Gray (1986) believes there are no inherent barriers to the drive derivatives, which he portrays as constantly seeking access to consciousness. If a resistance develops, it is the result of a conflict in action, and this is the moment when the resistance can be fruitfully brought to the patient's attention. Thus, the therapist must wait until that moment when there is evidence of the unconscious ego blocking unconscious drive derivatives before proceeding.

Inherent within this position is a view of an ego that is more passive than Schafer's or Apfelbaum and Gill's view. From this come questions about the ego's ability to observe its own resistances. Are there changes throughout an analysis so that one might need to stay closely attuned to the moment of resistance at one time, but at other times let the resistance and associations to it flourish so that a more subtle resistance interpretation might develop? From another perspective, can Schafer's concerns about focusing on the resistances be blunted, as Gray might suggest, via education without becoming intellectualized?

These are examples of some of the questions that need to be investigated over time. What is exciting is that the early promise of ego psychology seems finally to be bearing fruit in these investigations on the resistances. Meaningful questions on the role of the ego in clinical technique are being addressed. However, we must also not get too far ahead of ourselves. As noted in the initial section of this chapter, there are still those who view resistances from a drive-dominated position. For some the ego resistances are still a barrier to be breached so that the unconscious drive derivatives behind them can be uncovered.

Writing contemporaneously with those authors just noted, Dewald (1980) starts from the premise that core resistances (what he calls "strategic resistances") exist to aid in the maintenance of unconscious gratifications and the avoidance of painful feelings associated with *renunciation of these gratifications*. Dewald sees the ego functioning in what he calls "tactical resistances," which are used to defend against awareness of strategic resistances. Although Dewald does not discuss why it is necessary to defend against strategic resistances, it would seem that this action is because of the *pain and grief the patient would feel if he or she became aware of and needed to give up unconscious wishes*. However, what we see in Dewald's definition of ego defenses is that the ego part is relegated to a secondary role (i.e., protecting the unconscious wishes). A major clinical problem such a position poses is that it takes the clinician's view from the ego during a time of resistance to the unconscious wishes. In such a stance, one is drawn to bypass the ego resistances to get to the unconscious libidinal component of the resistances.

Thus, once again we see an experienced clinician taking a position on the meaning of ego resistances that would likely lead to them being bypassed. It reflects a regressive view of patients in which an enfeebled ego is there primarily to protect and guard the infantile wishes. The notion that infantile wishes continue to exist, in part, because of the fear associated with higher-level functioning leads us again to recognize that it is, specifically, the threat to the ego that remains unacknowledged here. Why Dewald might come to this position in contrast to Gray and the others will be explored next.

DISCUSSION

Why do we need to keep rediscovering a way to work with resistances that takes into account the latter stages of Freud's thinking on anxiety? There are numerous factors that must be considered in order to understand this phenomenon. Some are historic, some seem to be hazards of the profession.

To start with, Freud's new theory of anxiety did not lead him to any radical rethinking on the technique of resistance interpretation. While phrases from his pre-1926 approach to resistances give the impression of a growing understanding consistent with the new theory of the role of the ego in resistances, reading the entire text allows one to see the primacy of Freud's early theory of anxiety. In fact, Strachey (1959) notes that as Freud expounded on the correctness of his new theory of anxiety, he did not fully abandon the first theory of anxiety. Brenner (1982) points out that Freud needed to keep a purely economic, quantitative explanation for anxiety to explain what he saw as "contentless anxiety" in the actual neurosis. Thus, even while refuting his old theory, Freud (1926) states, "[W]e see, then, that it is not so much a question of taking back our earlier findings as of bringing them into line with more recent discoveries" (p. 141). The student of psychoanalysis in 1926, then, was left with a confusing picture on the causes of resistances. The technical approach to resistances based upon economic principles would be quite different from that based on an unconscious sense of danger. The approach to the actual neurosis necessitated a freeing of the repressed drive, while the second theory of anxiety required a careful exploration of the perceived dangerous affects that set off the resistances. These very different approaches continue to find their way into the literature on resistances. While few psychotherapists would agree today with a view of anxiety based on a dammed-up libido, the impact of this view has remained significant in the clinical literature and has left some with the impression that Freud was ambivalent about the ego's role in resistances (Gray 1982).

The continued emphasis on the primacy of drives in Freud's view of resistances can be seen in the following quote:

> The dynamic factor which makes a working-through of this kind necessary and comprehensible is not far to seek.

> It must be that after the ego-resistance has been removed
> the power of the compulsion to repeat—the attraction
> exerted by the unconscious prototypes upon the repressed
> instinctual process—has still to be overcome. [Freud 1926,
> p. 159]

One can see in this passage Freud's view of the power of the
drives as an important component in the working through
process. From the side of the ego, however, one can say that
working through is necessary to explore the unconscious
threats to the ego. Indeed, if one sees working-through as a
battle against the attraction of the unconscious drives, special techniques are necessary to keep the conscious ego's
attention on the resistance and to bolster the patient's attempt to fight off the power of the unconscious gratifications.
Therefore, arguments against the resistances, along with
"rewards and advantages" proposed to the ego if it gives up
its resistances, are logical extensions of this economic view of
the resistances. This view of the resistances, as something to
be overcome via the use of what we would now call special
parameters, has had a profound effect on psychoanalytic
perspectives on the resistances. As Gray (1986) notes:

> [T]he positive transference . . . is a form of suggestion that
> is still widely used to overcome resistance. It is usually
> more accepted in practice than acknowledged in theory.
> Many analyzable patients have a capacity and a tendency
> to cling to this particular motivational source. Analysts
> who depend on it usually assume it will be relinquished
> near the end of the analysis. This is not necessarily the
> case. [p. 247]

Another possible reason for our clinical stagnation in
approaching the resistances is that the earliest and most
influential ego psychologists, following Freud's predilection
for theory building, were more interested in the ego as part of
a general psychology. Many analysts (Apfelbaum 1962,
Arlow 1975, Fogel 1989) have noted that the work of these
theorists was criticized for being remote from clinical experi-

ence. Thus, the beginning explorations of the dimensions of the ego were not clinical in nature but instead turned toward the development of the ego, its autonomous functioning, and especially developmental tasks in conjunction with the environment and their effect on the ego. This line of investigation has germinated a rich harvest of data that ultimately has enriched our clinical work. However, the more strictly clinical investigations into the work of the ego, especially the unconscious ego, have suffered from benign neglect. The result has been that our knowledge of the resistances, as Weinshel (1984) notes, has stagnated. Our clinical work suffers from confusing messages on the correct technique for dealing with resistances, and the more interesting questions in dealing with resistances still need to be addressed.

I believe we also need to look in a direction other than our intellectual educational past to discover the reasons for our neglect of the resistances. The region we need to explore further has to do with the pleasures, disappointments, and hazards of the profession. Stone (1973) and Gray (1982) have described the power or magnetism of the id for most therapists in contrast to the resistances. To support this opinion, all I would ask is for the reader to think back to his or her last discussion of clinical case material and recall how many of the comments were directed to the "real" unconscious fantasy (especially if the analysis was stalled). While each of us has unique personal reasons for this predilection to interpret one particular type of material over another, when an entire group shows this tendency, we are dealing with more than an individual phenomenon. The search for a hidden, driving force behind seemingly random events is as old as humankind itself, and it is a motivational source for the development of religion and the sciences. To find behind people's suffering a secret, unifying theme that touches on our basic nature is the stuff of human dreams from the beginning of time. The psychotherapist's tendency to search for the unconscious fantasy binding together the symptoms, transferences, external reality, and daydreams of the patient is the psychotherapist engaging in an endeavor that has always captivated us. However, while scientists and philosophers may spend lifetimes searching for a small piece of the answer to the great human mysteries, we often feel we come up with our answers daily, if not several times in one day, if we are really cooking. In this context, it is interesting to remember that Oedipus's marriage to Jocasta was preceded by two important events. One was the killing of Laius; the other was solving the riddle of the Sphinx. This tale has led me to wonder whether, in part, our attraction to unraveling the mysteries of the unconscious id is a repetition of this timeless ritual, with the fantasy reward and attendant feelings of power, a revival of the wished-for oedipal victory.

A number of other factors tend to draw us away from the resistances. When a patient is in the throes of a prolonged resistance, the "feeling in the session" is that the patient is working against the therapist. For most of us, this situation raises issues of narcissistic injury and attendant anger during which time we are not at our most empathic. Furthermore, it is at a time when the patient is most resolute in fighting the analysis and therapist, often outside of his or her awareness, in a way the patient is frequently comfortable with. It is at these times that we need to be most empathic with our patient's earliest anxieties and fears of being overwhelmed. Thus, when the patient is most out of tune with the idealized analytic state that serves as a model for participation, we need to be most understanding of the patient's primitive affective states. This understanding then needs to be integrated and presented to the patient in a way that is not threatening.

We also need to consider whether our desire to explain the meanings behind the resistance, before exploring the resistance itself, is an attempt to defend against both the patient's primitive anxieties and our own hostility by being "overgiving." As with any need to be "giving," one has to wonder about the unconscious hostility behind such an act. In fact, it is not infrequent for patients to associate to violent intrusions, or to become more masochistic after a resistance has been bypassed with an interpretation of the unconscious wishes behind it. Furthermore, the intellectualization inherent in interpreting before the resistance has been clarified and the affect explored seems to be the therapist's way of defending against the depth of feeling associated with resistances that initially appear wordless or as "action thoughts" (Busch 1989). In the throes of a resistance, even our higher functioning patients seem more primitive.

Finally, I do not believe we have had a good language for exploring the resistances. Just as with those patients with whom putting things into words brings an alteration in higher-level ego functions (Loewald 1971), the same can be said for clinical concepts. While most therapists know that interpretations of resistances should take place first, exactly what this means, how it might be done, and what one needs to look for still seem like a few of our prime current methodological mysteries. As Gray (1986) notes, Freud's observation on the resistance to uncovering resistances "often results from the analyst's failure to provide the analysand with the best opportunity to perceive the resistance" (p. 254).

Gray's articles on techniques for helping patients learn about unconscious ego resistances are an excellent beginning in this area. However, it may not have been sufficiently emphasized that understanding resistances might take a slightly different type of listening on the therapist's part. In most case reports, one hears the therapist listening to the *content* of the associations for the derivatives of the unconscious fantasies. Listening for the resistances sometimes requires greater attention to the *process* of associations. The heart of Gray's clinical technique revolves around listening for the moment in the psychoanalytic process when a resistance is in operation. He has called these moments "breaking points" (1990, p. 1087) in which there is a change in voice. "It may be a blatant, dramatic sudden difference from what occupies the moment before; or it may be an exceedingly subtle alternative" (p. 1087). Gray (1991) has likened this process to the therapist functioning as an apple picker watching a conveyer belt for bad apples. At other times, one can hear the resistance in a patient's "consistency of voice"—

for example, the patient who rushes from topic to topic in order to ward off a fantasy of being suffocated, or the patient who keeps spaces between every topic so they do not touch. At these times, the therapist may listen primarily for the meaning of *how* the patient is associating rather than the meaning of the associations themselves. The associations may be in the action of associating. While this is likely a familiar manner of listening for many therapists, like the resistances themselves, familiarity should not breed content.

6

ACTIONS AND ANALYSIS

Loewald's (1971, 1975) prescient observations on the role of action in the psychoanalytic process are succinctly captured in his statement that "we take the patient less and less as speaking merely about himself, about his experiences and memories, and more and more as symbolizing *action in speech*, as speaking from the depths of his memories, which regain life and poignancy by the impetus and urgency of reexperience in the present of the analytic situation" (1975, p. 366, italics added).

Action is ubiquitous throughout treatment, and the traditional distinctions between words and actions can be limiting and erroneous. Verbalization itself is increasingly being seen as a form of action (Boesky 1982, Chused 1991, Roughton, in press). As evocatively captured by McLaughlin (1991), words "become acts, things—sticks and stones, hugs and holdings" (p. 598). Thus, the patient who struggles to express some perfunctory associations in response to telling a dream may be found to be extending his raised middle finger toward the therapist with the unspoken admonition "This is a dream about 'normal' activities and couldn't possibly have meaning." Further observation may reveal that overt attempts at bumbled compliance mask a defiance toward those seen in positions of power, expressed in this manner as an adaptation to parents whose capacity for largesse was experienced as fragile and dependent on their not being challenged.

Such is the fare of many analytic hours. The "action" here is not of an overt type (i.e., motoric act, postural or facial change, etc.). In the patient's manner of associating, he or she is doing something (which is the dictionary definition of an action). While the words are compliant, the action in the words are the opposite. However, only by paying attention to why the material is presented in this form (i.e., action) can we approach an interpretive strategy that is useful to patients and consistent with analytic technique and that takes into account our understanding of the ego. The debate in our literature on this point has not been vigorous, with rudimentary views of action and verbalization limiting our vision.

Some analytic hours have much to do with action, and some have much to do with words. The most powerful, from the patient's perspective, are when actions and words come together in the action of the transference and are understood as one. Some analyses have more to do with words, but it is hard to imagine a fully evolved transference (both resisted and experienced) without actions. On the other hand, it is difficult, if not impossible, to conduct most of an analysis in the context of ongoing actions. Certain types of thought processes, usually expressed in words, are the *sine qua non* of an analytic process having taken place. However, throughout most of our analytic history, we have mistakenly judged actions as entirely antagonistic to the psychoanalytic process. This is most succinctly captured in the pejorative manner that the term *acting out* was employed to label almost any behavior not obedient to the fundamental rule. Furthermore, this label was used not as a beginning exploration of the action in question but rather as an admonition intended to get the patient back to talking (as if talking in itself could not be an action).

Many forms of action take place in the analytic setting. There are the subtle forms alluded to by Loewald, in which the words become the action (e.g., the manner of associating to a dream is a denial of its meaning). There are the characteristic actions (e.g., the patient who lumbers or flies into the office), and postures (e.g., head, torso, and extremities are usually aligned in a particular manner, indicating the patient's stance in relation to the therapist that day). There are actions taken outside the analytic hour that are directly related to the analysis, such as forgetting a session, skipping a session, or losing the bill, and motoric acts within the hour such as changes in position on the couch, sitting up, or leaving the hour.

Freud's (1914) beginning forays into this area (i.e., actions as the patient's only way of remembering but also as a resistance to remembering) seem initially contradictory, but in actuality they are a subtle rendering of the complexities needed to comprehend actions. Freud understood that at times it was the action of the transference that needed the most attention.

> For instance, the patient does not say that he remembers
> that he used to be defiant and critical towards his parents'
> authority; instead, he behaves in that way to the doctor. He
> does not remember how he came to a helpless and hopeless
> deadlock in his infantile sexual researches; but he pro-
> duces a mass of confused dreams and associations, com-
> plains that he cannot succeed in anything and asserts that
> he is fated never to carry through what he undertakes. He
> does not remember having been intensely ashamed of
> certain sexual activities and afraid of their being found out;
> but he makes it clear that he is ashamed of the treatment
> on which he has now embarked and tries to keep it secret
> from everybody. [p. 150]

Freud's clinical insights into actions as the patient's only way of remembering, or as a resistance to remembering, were soon overtaken by changes in Freud's thinking that severely altered these perspicacious observations. Thus, the clinical reality that patients are bound to repeat their conflicts in the action of the analysis became linked with a quality of an instinct, and eventually with the ill-fated concept of the death instinct. Furthermore, as noted in previous chapters, Freud's ambivalence toward the resistances as something to be overcome versus understood led, for many years, to a delay in our understanding of resistances. Within this context, actions as resistances became something the ego was induced to give up by promising it "rewards and advantages" (Freud 1926, p. 159). Thus, action began increasingly to be seen by therapists in malignant terms as its resistance features became connected with self-destructive tendencies. As characterized by Grinberg (1968):

> There are some terms in the psychoanalytical literature the mere mention of which awakens a penumbra of associations tinged with a specific significance. This meaning sometimes overshadows any other content implicit in the context. The term acting out happens to be one of them and it often carries a pejorative connotation denoting the so-called "bad " behavior that characterizes some patients in analysis. [p. 171]

For many years, then, action as the patient's "only way of remembering" faded into the background as a tenet of analytic communication. Our views on development, as well as the analytic process, became dominated by concepts relying heavily on quantitative assessments of verbalizations. This position was heavily influenced by Freud's (1915) overly dichotomized views on how thoughts become conscious (i.e., word presentations become connected with thing presentations), in the context of a mistaken model of energy transfers accruing to thoughts based on their systemic placement. As a result, the method of free association became based on the patient's ability to verbalize thoughts, while their ability to use thoughts for self-analysis faded into the background.

From a developmental perspective, verbalization was

touted as the royal road to integrating reality testing and the secondary process (Katan 1961). Development was sharply divided between preverbal and verbal periods (usually around 12–18 months), while the vast difference in use, meaning, and quantity of words during the first years of life remained ignored. Changes in qualities of thought processes, relatively independent of language development, remained disregarded. Until the significance of action was resuscitated by Loewald, "there [had] been a strong tendency to exclude action, both in fact and theory, from this mostly verbal process and to consider it a troublesome interference" (Roughton, in press).

What has been overlooked is that changes in analysis may be more fruitfully looked at through the prism of *quality of thought processes*. A simple example, mentioned earlier in these essays, may convey this point. By the end of analysis one would hope that a patient, caught in the throes of a transference, would move from being convinced that an impression of the therapist's greeting as less than exuberant was an indication of the *therapist's* mood toward the patient, to at least considering this as a possible sign of an important observation relative to the *patient's* mind. The significance of this step is that the patient moves from thinking of his or her thoughts only as realities, to thinking that can take itself as the object of its own inquiry. This change in orientation, which is a crucial component of self-analysis, matches certain developmental steps in thinking as it moves from its roots in action. The next section will follow this developmental line in preparation for understanding the role of action in the therapeutic process and its implications for technique. Throughout, my major premise is that the role of the ego has been overlooked in attempts to understand action in the psychoanalytic situation.

ACTION AS A DEVELOPMENTAL BASE OF THINKING

As I have indicated elsewhere (Busch 1989), thought is under the domination of action for a much longer period of time than has generally been recognized in psychoanalysis. Piaget (Piaget and Inhelder 1959) believes it is not until a child is around age 7 that one can talk of that child having an integrated cognitive system with which he or she can organize the world relatively free from action referents. Before that time, the child's thinking is heavily influenced by its motoric underpinnings. For example, a 5-year-old can successfully walk to school and negotiate a number of school corridors to find his kindergarten class, but he is unable to reproduce this in representational form as his thinking is of a "doing" type. The younger the child, the more his or her thinking will be dominated by action. For children capable of higher level functioning, conflict and regression will heighten the tendency toward thinking based on action.

> The reason for this "action type" of thinking has to do with the way thought processes develop. For example, Piaget believes that one of the major characteristics of all intelligence is that it is a matter of action. The main distinction between different stages of intellectual development is the degree to which actions become internalized and behavior is based upon representations rather than overt actions. However, it is important to note that the process of internalization is a very lengthy one. [Busch 1989, p. 538]

Child therapists have been aware of the the predominance of action in children's thinking for some time. For example, in discussing the mode of presenting material in child analysis, A. Freud stated on numerous occasions (1946, 1965a, Sandler et al. 1980) that it is age-appropriate that the child *acts* instead of talks. As recently expressed by Downey (1987), "On entering the analytic consulting room, most young children almost immediately turn to action and play to express their inner lives and their conflicts with the outer world. . . . Children intuitively and aggressively seek action outlets" (p. 106). The fact that children think in action terms is basic to those techniques developed for child analysis (i.e., play therapy) that allow children to communicate in the only form available to them: action. Central to my thesis, and as pointed out by Ritvo (1978), the *quality* of the child's thought processes limits the manner of interpretation and how the child can use his or her own material.

During the first 18 months of life, all the child's behaviors are guided by overt actions. While undergoing a remarkable development during this time, learning is of a trial and error type in interaction with environment. This type of thought processes "are sensory motor actions; thus, thought and action are identical at this time" (Wolff 1967, p. 324). It will be many years before the child's thinking is separated from its sensory-motor beginnings, and the child will develop "adaptations which require him to think and talk about reality rather than to act upon it directly" (Flavell 1963, p. 149).

In the next stage of development, lasting until around age 7 (preoperational stage), the child's thinking is guided increasingly by internal representations. Yet the internal life of the child during this stage still bears the marks of the sensory-motor period and is still tied to action. Thus, while the child shows a growing ability to represent reality, these representations are much closer to overt actions than for adults. When asked to convey an impression of the world around her, the child in this stage will impress us with the domination of action in her thought processes (Piaget 1930), while her definitions of words are grounded in action terms. A bike is "something you ride on," an umbrella is something "you put up when it rains," and so forth. As Flavell (1963) notes:

> The writer favors thinking of pre-operational thoughts as thought which bears the impress of its sensory-motor origins, that is, as saturated with sensory motor adherences. It is extremely concrete, its image signifiers even being more like internal replicas of concrete actions than true signs. . . . In short, in more respects than not, it simply resembles sensory-motor action which has simply been transposed to a new arena of operation. There is nothing extraordinary about this fact. Representations do not rise *ex nihilo*; born of a refined and developed sensory motor intelligence, it would be extraordinary if representational

thought did not resemble it at least in the beginning. [p. 162]

It is not until the child is around age 7 that he begins to approach the world with a more balanced cognitive system (stage of concrete operations).

> Much more than his younger counterpart, he gives the decided impression of possessing a solid cognitive bedrock, something flexible and plastic and yet consistent and enduring, with which he can *structure the present in terms of the past without undue strain and dislocation,* that is, without the ever-present tendency to tumble into perplexity and contradiction which mark the preschooler. [Flavell 1963, p. 165, emphasis added]

Shapiro and Perry (1976), after reviewing a diverse sampling of the developmental literature, note the significant stabilization of cognitive structures at this time. Child therapists see a changeover to the primacy of more verbal forms of communication around age 7 or 8 (Sandler et al. 1980). However, during this stage the child's thinking is still concrete and organized toward events in the immediate present. It is not for a few years that we see the capacity to go beyond classifying and organizing just what comes to the senses. The older child can move beyond the real to deal with what is possible.

> No longer exclusively preoccupied with the sober business of trying to stabilize and organize just what comes directly to the senses, the adolescent has, through this new orientation, the potentiality of imagining all that might be there—both the very obvious and the very subtle—and thereby of much better insuring the finding of all that is there. [Flavell 1963, p. 205]

IMPLICATIONS FOR TECHNIQUE

Freud's (1914) view on the ubiquity of action in analysis is echoed by Loewald (1975):

In the course of the psychoanalytic process, narrative is drawn into the context of transference dramatization, in the force-field of re-enactment. Whether in the form of free associations or of more consciously, logically controlled trains of thought, narrative in psychoanalysis is increasingly being revealed in its character as language action, as symbolic action and in particular as language action within the transference force field. The reference in regard to content and emotional tone of the communication through narrative, shifts more and more to their relevance as transference repetitions and transference actions in the psychoanalytic situation. One might express this by saying we take the patient less and less as speaking merely *about* himself, about his experiences and memories, and more and more as symbolizing action in speech, as speaking from the depth of his memories, which regain life and poignancy by the impetus and the urgency of re-experience in the present of the analytic situation. [pp. 293–294]

Action becomes increasingly woven into the fabric of the psychoanalytic process for a number of reasons. What has not been emphasized sufficiently is that one important factor has to do with the *long period of time that the child's thinking is under the influence of action determinants.* Central conflicts and the adaptations to them are first experienced, thought about, and worked out at an *action* level. Whatever the danger, the original defensive adaptations and compromise formations were undertaken in action terms and thus may remain unavailable to higher-level ego functioning or remain in waiting as regressive flash points.

What I have tried to point out in this paper is that, for a much longer time than we have been aware of in psychoanalysis, children's thoughts are "action" dominated. Up until the oedipal phase and its crucial importance in shaping psychic development, action-tendencies remain as a primary mode of the child's thought processes. During this time the conflicts that arise and the methods used to cope with these are dominated by the action patterns of the pre-operational child. [Busch 1989, p. 542]

A. Freud (1968) reminds us that neurotic conflicts and their solutions are a constant force in the individual's psychic makeup and that regressive expression is encouraged by analytic technique. Furthermore, in response to the inevitable anxiety and dangers experienced by the patient as the transference neurosis deepens, regressions encompassing earlier forms of adaptation are inevitable. It should not surprise us that in this situation, compromises based on earlier forms of thinking will appear.

Child therapists tend to see adults' action tendencies as resulting from experiences occurring at an early age not becoming part of the organized ego, and thus they "cannot be 'remembered,' only relived within the transference" (A. Freud 1965, p. 32). Or, as Downey (1987) has put it, "The earlier in life the memory arises in the older child or adult, the more likely it has to be recovered by being made manifest through *action* or art as an adjunct to words" (p. 106, italics added). Sandler (1975) cogently argues there is a way of thinking, organized according to childhood laws of perception and cognition, that continues to operate in the present outside of consciousness. Thus, what persists into adulthood is not only the content of past memories and fantasies but also structures representing ways of making connections, conceptions of causality, the absence of chance events, and so forth. She believes that psychoanalysis has tended to neglect the information that can be provided by a knowledge of the "*dominant modes of unconscious childhood cognition which persist in the present and which are still utilized in the present*" (p. 376, emphasis original).

While future research might look for specific qualities associated with the multiple causes of action tendencies (i.e., regressive ego functioning, re-creation of unconscious childhood cognition, spontaneous creation of the neurosis using an earlier form of thinking for a variety of purposes), what I am focusing on is the ubiquity of action, its similarities to earlier forms of thinking, and the implications of this for technique. The following is a typical example of action in the analytic setting.

A middle-aged woman, after associating for a period of

time, would frequently say, "I don't know" before returning to her thoughts. Over a long period of time, the following pattern emerged. When the patient said, "I don't know," she was saying, "What I have just said means nothing." This was an attempt to bait the therapist into an argument on the merits of free association in the hopes of angering him, with the fantasy that the therapist would then feel guilty and attempt to make it up to the patient. This was a repetition of an ongoing childhood experience. Her parents were divorced when she was 3, and she would spend Saturday with her father. She would sit in a particular chair and play with the nap of the material while watching television. This behavior would anger the father, leading him to raise his voice in exasperation. The patient would start to sob, which led the father to hug her, and the rest of the day would pass tranquilly.

All this came to mind when the patient became increasingly aware of longings toward the therapist, while also sensing the therapist's frustration (before he did) with these beginning oppositional battles. With the phrase "I don't know," the patient attempted to enact with the therapist: a beating fantasy that had elements of oedipal triumph and guilt; an attempt to turn her father's frightening anger from something passively experienced into something actively brought on; a sadistic fantasy of getting the therapist to lose control of his temper, like her father, which she experienced as exciting; and an expression of anger toward her father. The words "I don't know" were not primarily an expression of an internal state of ignorance but rather an unconscious action designed to actualize, defend against, and adapt to certain fantasies and realities that had been repeatedly enacted with her father. It is a subtle example of the manner in which words become actions. The fact that these ideas were expressed in action form has potentially important implications for technique that need to be considered.

Action Determinants in Thoughts

What follows are thoughts about clinical technique based upon action as a function of preoperational-type thinking. I am not suggesting that all actions that occur in psychoanalysis are the result of thinking unchanged from its preoperational roots. However, I am suggesting it is useful, in considering action to think of its formation in early thinking as a factor to be taken into account.

At its simplest level, the closer behavior is to pure action, the less accessible it is to usable information unless commented on by the patient. The manner in which a patient walks into the hour or lies on the couch represents complex compromise formations kept at the level of action, in part, for defensive reasons. While it may represent information to the therapist, it is not necessarily an intended *communication* from the patient. It is at a level of thought that the patient's analyzing ego cannot use. This is why, in my experience, patients are invariably caught off guard by comments on behaviors that are closer to actions. By doing this, we are *circumventing layers of resistances* that have led the behavior to stay at an action level, where the patient's capacity to reflect back on him- or herself is very limited.

It has been my impression from examining my tendencies, listening to the work of colleagues, and reading the literature that the proclivity to interpret actions prematurely occurs when there is an impasse in the treatment brought about by a central resistance. The therapist knows they are in the midst of an important resistance, often of a prolonged nature, when the action is interpreted as a type of secret unconscious key that will unlock the resistance. This is evident in Deutsch's (1947, 1952) classic papers in posturology. While in his early paper he cites the danger of prematurely drawing the patient's attention to motoric behavior, at a later time he champions the advantage of directing free association to posture, especially when the *"resistance unduly delays progress"* (1952, p. 212, italics added). The dilemma of recognizing that actions need to be approached cautiously, while at the same time trying to break an impasse in the treatment by prematurely interpreting actions, is not a thing of the past, as judged by recent literature on the topic. "A consistent analytic approach to Mr. B's various expressions of nonverbal behavior, i.e., his specific motor movements and postures, *became a potent remedy against a threatening deadlock in the analysis"* (Anthi 1983, p. 46, italics added).

Understanding the meaning of a patient's action in the context of a treatment impasse will, no doubt, be of some eventual help to the analysis. The question is in what way? To use this understanding to make an interpretation, in order to break an impasse, usually has little impact, at best. A typical example of a patient's response to such an attempt is captured by McLaughlin (1987):

> One day I asked him to reflect upon his raised hands, as he talked about his father. He professed to be unaware and *could develop no associations, even when I pressed with questioning about a possible relation between the two.* [p. 566, italics added]

It seems more likely that the progress McLaughlin reports in this case comes from *his* understanding of this behavior, in the contextual framework of the rest of the case, than the specific interpretation of the behavior. In fact, most approaches to the interpretations of actions suffer from the persistent influence of the topographic model on our theory of technique. We continue to labor under the notion that if we can only make conscious the unconscious fantasy fueling the action, the therapeutic stalemate will be ended.

Our attempt to understand action is almost entirely focused on content, with only a passing nod to the issue of the therapeutic implications of the *form of the behavior*. The question of what it says about the level of the patient's ego functioning, and his or her ability to hear our interpretations, that he or she is "speaking" to us in actions, seems relatively ignored. As I shall argue shortly, I believe this issue has profound effects on how we can interpret. Suffice it to say at this point that in order to ask the question, the analytic material must be approached, in part, from the side of the ego and the structural model. Using only genetic reconstructions of why patients express themselves in action form (e.g., Meyers's [1987] comprehensive listing of genetic factors leading his patients toward action — strain trauma, identification with the aggressor, battles over autonomy, etc.) seems a less fruitful line of approach toward understanding action than one that takes into account its ubiquitousness throughout all analyses and the implications of this state for understanding more about ego functioning and resistance analysis. Yet it has been the dynamic and genetic interpretations of actions that have prevailed.

Further complicating matters is the difficulty of evaluating the effect of our interventions. If we view our interpretations within the framework of "destabilizing the equilibrium of forces of conflict" (Arlow and Brenner 1990, p. 680), an initial negative reaction can be explained away if some ultimate positive effect occurs. This seems to be the course followed by most authors discussing direct interpretations of actions that, at the time, seem to be circumventing a resistance. They report an initial negative reaction before a generally positive one (à la McLaughlin, discussed earlier). The initial negative reaction can be rationalized within the context of the positive trend of treatment. However, in these cases what is due to an analytic process rather than suggestion or resorting to authority is difficult to determine. McLaughlin (1991) seems to recognize this implicitly when he describes his work with enactments as increasingly based on "less assertion of personal bias and steering" (p. 612).

If an action is noted by the patient, we see a readiness to observe behavior already indicative of higher-level ego functioning ready to be applied to the action. As with other types of communications, patients may signal a readiness to explore actions without directly commenting upon them. In such situations, I always find it best to preface my observation about their action with a question like, "Are you aware that. . . ?" or "Have you noticed. . . ?" By focusing on the patient's observational inclinations it allows the patient to use this skill or not, depending on his or her wishes, with less of the sense of embarrassment associated with making an interpretation of an action without taking into account the patient's ability to be aware of it. If there is no awareness of the action, there is no observing ego to look back upon it with any degree of curiosity as to its meaning.

The following example illustrates how an action can be put into words after a resistance is focused on first, rather than the more common form described earlier (i.e., an action interpreted to break through a resistance). Mr. A. came into a session feeling discouraged. He complained that we kept talking about the same old stuff, that he never got any deeper into his feelings, and that he ought to start thinking about terminating the treatment. As he was saying this, I noted that his right foot was gently touching a plant at the end of the couch in a rhythmic fashion. I could not remember this happening before. As Mr. A. became more morose about his progress, I both sympathized with his concerns and wondered about his reluctance to consider these as "thoughts" he was having, as he had in the past. With an edge in his voice, he parried this with his belief that he had come to certain reality realizations and that it would be foolish to consider these as anything else. I commented on how it sounded like there was an edge in his voice and wondered whether he could tell me what it was about. He said that while he felt he was talking about reality, I was suggesting that his thoughts meant something else. He then began a harangue against me for overinterpreting, when things were sometimes just what they were. Upon completion he breathed deeply, laughed, and said,"I feel a lot better now." He then noted that while talking he remembered an incident at work last week when a co-worker, right before leaving for vacation, had managed to piss everyone off. He then remembered that we were two weeks from a week-long break in the treatment. In his heart, he said, he wanted to fight with me about the meaning of this incident. At this point, he noted the rhythmic touching of the plant with his foot. He wondered, with some sadness in his voice, whether this was an expression of a wish to get close and wondered why it was so difficult for him to know about these wishes.

In this example we have a motor action expressing a wish in a highly defended form that, when the verbal form of the resistance is focused on, can spontaneously come to the patient's mind. I have found this a useful process to keep in mind as a model for the exploration of actions. In this case, two simultaneous action resistances are going on. While the patient is talking as if his thoughts were only realities, he is using a motor action to express a wish and to defend against awareness of that wish. It is also an example of Apfelbaum and Gill's (1989) reminder "that what is defense at one moment in relation to a given wish may the next moment become the wish defended against" (p. 1076). Thus, Mr. A,'s use of his right foot to express a wish to be close with me was a highly overdetermined act.

It was many years into the analysis before Mr. A. could tell me that it wasn't until his forties that he was able to buy his own clothes, including shoes. Up until that time, it was his mother who purchased his clothes for him, and then his wife. His ability to feel manly was severely interfered with, as exemplified by masturbatory fantasies of being a woman with a penis while wearing woman's undergarments. He had a compulsive ritual in which his becoming aware of a mannerism on one side of his body led him to need to do the same thing with the other side. So if he was rubbing two fingers together on his right hand, he would then have to do the same thing with his left hand. It was always the left side that would need to be included after noticing that he had done something with his right side. He associated his right side with masculinity and the left side with femininity. Thus, in the action with his foot, it was significant that it was his right foot only that was touching the plant.

Mr. A. had no male friends, was generally dismissive of most men, and had been especially disparaging toward his father. Throughout the analysis he had often moved his feet from side to side, in unison, in what was a symbolic replication of a car windshield wiper. This was associated with wiping away any feelings of connection with me as a male, while also wiping away the water (tears) from his sadness over his self-isolation. Fighting was, at times, the only form of contact Mr. A. could allow himself with me.

One can see the rich dynamic and genetic significance associated with Mr. A.'s use of his foot, and this aspect has been what has generally been focused on in the literature. However, what I have been impressed with is how we as therapists seem to need to be reminded to pay attention to and respect the defenses. This is why I have highlighted the defense aspects of actions. Furthermore, it is what has been deemphasized in the literature on action in adult analysis. What I am suggesting technically is that when an action is in operation, its possibility as a resistance using an earlier form of thinking needs to be considered. I am not suggestiong that all actions that occur in psychoanalysis are the result of thinking unchanged from its preoperational roots. However, I am suggesting it is useful, in considering action, to think of its formation in early thinking as a factor to be taken into account. What is salient in the example is that the wish (to be close to a man) is expressed in a highly defended form (an action), and at the same time a similar resistance is occuring in a verbal form. Once the verbal resistance is understood by the patient, he is able to allow himself to become aware of the underlying wish expressed in the action defense.

This is the essence of what I am offering on understanding action. Its role as a resistance has been neglected, which has led us to miss the feeling of threat behind the action and the need to treat it as any other resistance. This is what I mean when I say the mode of expression needs to be taken into consideration. If an action is in operation, its resistance aspects encompassing preoperational thought need to be considered. The particular action will be overdetermined.

Qualities of Preoperational Thought

Germane to our interpretive efforts is the fact that there are certain qualities associated with preoperational thoughts. The first of these can be seen in the patient's total immersion in the affective truth of a transference reaction. In the midst of the transference neurosis, the one-second scan of the therapist's face upon initial greeting convinces the patient, without doubt, of the therapist's feeling of anger, contentment, self-absorption, and so forth. At these times there is frequently nothing else the patient believes necessary to consider or think about. There is no capacity to objectify his or her thinking at this point. Thus, the patient cannot think, "It is as if I had the impression of Dr. B. looking mad," but rather we see a reaction based upon a sense of certainty. At these times, the patient's thought processes are dominated by a particular quality characteristic of preoperational thought. As noted earlier, the person under the influence of preoperational thought

> feels neither the compunction to justify his reasoning to others nor to look for possible contradictions in his logic. He is, for example, unable to reconstruct a chain of reasoning which he has just passed through; he thinks but he cannot think about his thinking. [Flavell 1963, p. 156]

Most therapists would agree this is the level patients are thinking through much of analysis—they think but do not think about their thinking. Thoughts and feelings are not so much expressions of psychic reality, but just are.

Another characteristic typical of patients enmeshed in the transference neurosis is the immediacy of their thoughts. These individuals, who may be admired in their field for their bold, creative thinking, in the area of their conflicts become concrete and bound by immediate impressions. They cannot easily contemplate there is meaning to what is on their mind beyond its initial, knowable quality. As is typical of the preoperational child, thoughts are considered "*solely in terms of the phenomenal, before-the-eye reality*" (Flavell 1963, p. 203, italics added).

The implications of these observations are that interpretive efforts work best when connected to what is most *observable, concrete*, and thus knowable by the patient who is functioning at an earlier level of conceptual ability. Freud (1910) captured this when he described how an interpretation must be "in the neighborhood" of what the patient is thinking. In my elaboration of this concept (Busch 1993), I note that a patient must be able to make some connection between what he or she is thinking and the therapist's intervention. The brilliance of our understanding of the unconscious is simply not useful data until it can be connected to something the patient can be consciously aware of. While Freud eschewed this clinical line of thought under pressure from never-abandoned aspects of the topographic model, it remained central in the work of A. Freud (1936) and is highlighted by Gray (1982) when he states, *"[T]he therapeutic results of analytic treatment are lasting in proportion to the extent to which, during the analysis, the patient's unbypassed ego functions have become involved in a consciously and increasingly voluntary copartnership with the analyst"* (p. 624, italics origional).

Throughout an analysis, we must attempt to work with what is most tangible, knowable, and concrete to the patient. In order to do this, it is most helpful to stay within the here and now of the transference, within the context of the patient's tasks laid out in a straightforward manner with accommodations for appropriate timing. The patient's tasks are to say whatever comes to mind (with the recognition that this is not a task that can always be fulfilled) and to see thoughts as data that will help him or her understand conflicts. While I see this as what is essentially psychoanalytic about psychoanalysis, it is also difficult to concretize behavior in a collaborative manner unless these guidelines are set as the backdrop for the psychoanalytic process.

Essential, then, to a prototype for analyzing action is that there is a model of analysis within which the patient and I will be working, and anything that strays from this position will be an indication that there is potentially a resistance in action that will be helpful to consider. Without such guidelines, I have found no easy entry into collaborative efforts for analyzing actions. Thus, with most patients, wherever possible, entry into the analytic process of analyzing resistances in action would come with observations like "I wonder whether you noticed that after you had a critical thought about me, there was a pause and your thoughts became complimentary" or "After appearing interested in your initial thoughts and their meaning, you seem to be thinking of your thoughts as descriptions of everyday and not psychological events."

My purpose, then, is to concretize what is essential for a psychoanalysis to take place, while focusing attention some significant portion of the time on the resistances to these processes. It is a first level of entry into the action level at which compromises are taking place throughout the analysis. Most importantly, it is tangible, concrete behavior, which is easier to bring before the patient for consideration, without stretching the level of conceptualizing beyond what the patient can handle. As the concrete nature of resistances can be established with the patient, it is then possible to look at some of the subtle (but still concrete) forms of action that the resistances take. Thus, why a patient presents thoughts as entertaining, desperate, a chronology of the weekend, or a recitation of past traumas all become an entry into investigating a resistance in action to thoughts as reflections of internal psychological states. These can only be elaborated, over time, in the context of the tangible goals of psychoanalysis to say whatever comes to mind as a method of understanding internal psychological states.

Gray's method of close process monitoring, within the context of what he (1986) describes as the two methods of observation in analysis (i.e., observing that thoughts are occurring [free association] and observing these thoughts as expressions of intrapsychic states [self-observation]), serve as an ideal method for analysis of actions. Put most succinctly, it *concretizes* the analytic task and the patient's response to it at a time when his thinking is most concrete. When looked at in its essentials, the analytic process can be conceived as following what the patient is allowing into his or her mind, what is allowed to be connected with what, what arises as interferences with this, and what the patient is doing with thoughts while talking (i.e., thoughts as gifts, questions, demands, etc.). This becomes a different view of the process than the therapist as interpreter of "absent content" (Searl 1936), when the primary function of the analysis becomes the therapist's search for the unconscious fantasies in the figure of the patient's ground. Such methods are not as congruent with the patient's cognitive capabilities throughout much of an analysis. I believe this is one important factor in why so many of the patients we see in second analyses have intellectual insights into their problems that are of little help to them.

For a patient, during much of an analysis, hearing interpretations detached from concrete referents is like trying to learn to hit a baseball by watching films of Babe Ruth or Ted Williams. Until one has the experience of holding a bat, along with a feel for the intricate movements necessary to swing the bat successfully, studying the moves of the masters will have little significance because there will be no concrete referents in the individual's own experience. Being told by a batting instructor to watch how Ted Williams "keeps his head on the ball through the swing" might impress a person with the instructor's trove of batting esoterica, but it will mean little until facing a real ball being thrown at substantial speed. The fledgling batter needs to have a "memory in action" of the good-enough swing, along with some cognitive referents of the process, in order to make use of the coach's verbal instructions. The patient already has memories in action that need to have cognitive referents attached to them in concrete form so that he or she understands the process of learning. The best hitters in baseball can frequently look at a tape of themselves when they were hitting well and make the necessary adjustments in their swing in order to correct inevitable glitches. One way to conceptualize the results of follow-up studies of successful analyses (Schlessinger and Robbins 1983) is that patients develop the capacity to realize they have an internal videotape (free associations) that can be observed periodically to help deal with the mental glitches that are part of everyday life.

There are many components to an analysis: understanding of unconscious fantasies, understanding of the
present in terms of the past, empathic attunement with
relational variables both within and outside the analytic
session, a sense of appreciation for the struggle the patient is
engaged in, and so forth. Part of the art of psychoanalytic
technique is to know when resistances to the two components of the process (i.e., free association and self-observation) must be concretely pointed out and when there is
enough content expressed *through* the resistance that some
underlying dynamic can be pointed to in a way that is useful
to the patient. For example, when a patient is talking as if his
associations were primarily descriptions of external events, it
is an ongoing issue of analytic judgment (taking into account
innumerable variables) whether the external events themselves are a communication of what the resistances are about
or not. However, what psychoanalysis has to offer, in contrast
to other forms of treatment, is self-analysis. Its cornerstone is
the ability to allow thoughts to come to mind, while using
these thoughts as data that can be reviewed to see whatever
potential they might have for self-understanding. This deceptively modest goal, which captures a significant change in the
level of thinking, is the embodiment of thinking that has
moved from its *action roots in the preoperational phase.* I
believe it is the specific of what Loewald (1971) suggested as
the curative process in psychoanalysis in which experiences,
previously unavailable to higher-level ego functions, can now
be looked at via higher level thought processes with the
resulting freeing effect these processes have on the ability to
deal with experiences.

PART II

THE EGO
IN CONTEMPORARY
CLINICAL THOUGHT

7

SHADES OF GRAY

The work of Paul Gray demands serious attention from all students of psychoanalysis. In his compendious body of work, Gray resurrects and then instructs us in one of our basic concepts—the *resistances*. The state of disarray he has tried to lead us out of was succinctly captured by Schafer (1983) when he stated, "Certain things about resisting which ought to be well known, and are said to be well known and sufficiently appreciated and applied are in fact not well known enough and not consistently attended to in practice" (p. 66). Gray's (1982) felicitous term to describe this state of affairs was *developmental lag*, thus capturing the gap between our theoretical understanding of the centrality of resistances in analysis and our clinical grasp of how to analyze resistances.

A theoretical perspective for understanding the unconscious ego resistances was in place since 1926, after publication of "The Ego and the Id" (Freud 1923) and "Inhibitions, Symptoms, and Anxiety" (Freud 1926). It was at this point that we knew of the unconscious ego resistances and that anxiety was the result of a threat to the ego. What remained obscure was *how this understanding could be translated into meaningful clinical interventions, and toward what purpose.* Even after Freud realized the source of anxiety was in the unconscious ego's response to a perceived threat, he continued to base his clinical approach to the resistances on overcoming them via suggestion and influence: "we promise the ego rewards and advantages if it will give up its resistance" (Freud 1926, p. 159). In earlier papers when Freud described "working through" the resistances, he meant overcoming them through what we would now see as manipulation of the positive transference or support of the ego (Freud 1914, 1917b). Furthermore, even after Freud discovered that resistances could be unconscious, his clinical approach seemed to neglect the very fact that they were unconscious. His approach to resistances was not really to analyze them as we have come to learn about it. Instead, the resistances were seen as a barrier to be breached in order to unearth the drive derivatives as expressed in unconscious fantasies.

This perspective was a remnant of Freud's earlier views of anxiety as dammed-up libido and the topographic theory, with its emphasis on making the unconscious conscious by putting things into words (Freud 1900, 1915). It is another example of what Lear (1990) describes as the conflict between Freud the clinician, who could write sensitively as early as 1895 of the types of thoughts that caused resistances (e.g., "they were all of a distressing nature, calculated to arouse the affects of shame and self-reproach and of psychical pain, and the feeling of being harmed; they were all of a kind one would prefer to have not experienced, that one would rather forget"; [p.269]), and Freud the scientist, who tried to fit psychoanalysis within a particular scientific image. As noted earlier (Chapter 5), the resistances as a barrier to be overcome is a thematic undercurrent even in those who have otherwise contributed insights into the resistances, and it remains a typical underlying motif even in our most current definitions. It illustrates what Apfelbaum and Gill (1989) describe as a tendency among many therapists to view ego analysis as something preparatory to id analysis.

While psychoanalytic writers before Gray (Fenichel 1941, A. Freud 1936, Searl 1936) and contemporaneous with him (Kris 1982, 1983, 1990a,b, Schafer 1983, Weinshel 1984) expressed views similar to his on the resistances, no one had explored this topic in such depth. In Gray's view of the psychoanalytic process, resistance analysis is not undertaken as a prelude to something else. Rather, resistance analysis is at the center of the process. His views are steeped in the resistances as based on a threat to the ego, with access of thoughts to the conscious ego as a goal. Interest in his work stems, I believe, from his offering to the psychoanalytic clinician both an understanding of the nature of the resistances that fits with clinical experience, along with an explicit technique (a rarity itself) for working with resistances that makes intuitive and theoretical sense. His way of understanding one of our basic concepts also helps give shape and definition to the psychoanalytic process, and the work and goals of psychoanalysis become congruent. In Gray's view the goal of psychoanalysis is to aid the patient in continuing the work of psychoanalysis via the process of resistance analysis. In a larger sense, Gray's work is an application of an ego-psychological approach to psychoanalytic data, which heretofore has been sorely lacking in clinical applicability, with significant consequences for the direction of psychoanalytic technique and theory.

Thus, it is from a position of admiration and gratitude that I approach some of the underlying assumptions of Gray's technique for working with resistances. I believe additional perspectives could prove useful as adjuncts to Gray's point of view. The views I present are not an alternative to Gray's suggested technique and theoretical positions; rather they are questions and/or an additional slant that may offer the psychotherapist yet another perspective to add to his or her analytic armamentarium in understanding and working toward expansion of the ego via analysis.

CLOSE PROCESS MONITORING
AND THE FUNCTIONING OF THE EGO

The heart of Gray's clinical technique is his listening for the *moment* in the psychoanalytic process when a resistance is in operation, then bringing the patient's attention to it. One's attention is on the flow of the material, looking for some change that indicates that the flow of thoughts has been blocked. This is the *moment* of the resistance and the point at which the analysis of the resistances begins for Gray.

> One could call such a moment a "breaking point," in that the ego, resorting to a way of unconscious functioning developed for childhood purposes and now regressively repeated, does effect a "mini-breakdown" in mature functioning. At such moments, there is invariably a "change in voice" (R. Gardner, personal communication); of course "voice" here is used in its broadest connotations. It may be a blatant, dramatic sudden difference from what occupied the moment before; or it may be an exceedingly subtle alternative. In either case, it is a change that, with practice, is evident to a listening analyst's focus of attention. It does not depend on the analyst attending to his own unconscious. [1990, p. 1087]

What is immediately striking is Gray's emphasis on the *process* and his attunement to subtle changes in it as an expression of the resistances. This is in contrast to those therapists more oriented toward *content*.

A young man starts off his session talking of having had difficulty in falling asleep the previous evening. For a period of time he imagined he could hear his roommate having sex with the woman he brought home. He thought he heard the woman moaning in protest, and felt the roommate was being too pushy with her. There was then a brief pause. He then began a discussion of what a generally considerate fellow his roommate is.

A Grayian perspective on this vignette would lead the therapist to focus on the *moment of the brief pause*. He or she would bring the pause to the patient's attention (a necessary but frequently neglected first step) so that the patient's consciousness notices that a psychological mechanism has occurred; a break in the flow of thoughts took place. At some point the therapist might note with the patient that the pause was followed by a complimentary thought about the roommate, which was preceded by critical thoughts, adding that there may have been something threatening about these critical thoughts.

Note that in this case the therapist is focused primarily on the process as a vehicle for bringing the resistance to the patient's attention. The content is significant in that it is what might be resisted, but the emphasis in bringing in the content is the *threat* the patient felt under and not what the hostility was about. The possible primal scene meaning of the patient's hearing noises is not what would be significant to Gray at this point. Thus, what one see in Gray's work is that in order for the resistance to become part of the patient's conscious awareness, the process must be focused on. An operational definition that Gray proceeds under is that anything that interferes with the process of associations is a possible resistance.

Underlying Gray's method of close process monitoring for interpreting the resistances is a particular view of the ego. The three key elements of the ego in Gray's view are (1) drive derivatives that constantly seek access to consciousness; (2) no inherent barriers to these drive derivatives; and (3) if a resistance develops, it is the result of the ego experiencing anxiety and thus a developing conflict. "The crux of the difficulty in making the unconscious ego conscious is that the elements the analyst wants to bring into awareness are not 'driven' toward the patient's awareness, as are the id derivatives" (Gray 1986, p. 245). The therapist must wait for a sign that the unconscious ego is blocking the appearance of drive derivative material in order to proceed. "Once there is evidence that the patient has encountered a conflict over this trend, for which the ego initiates a form of resistance, my interest is in assessing if and how best I might be able to call the patient's attention to the event—the sequence—which has just taken place" (Gray 1990, p. 1086). Close process monitoring then becomes the ideal method for bringing the patient's attention to the resistances as they occur, in that at times other than active conflict, the resistances will not be observable by the patient. One cannot help a patient understand what he can have no awareness of, as is the case when the resistances are working silently (i.e., not intruding into the associative process). From this perspective, the therapist needs to wait and listen to the flow of associations until the moment when the resistance is observable.

> I regard as an optimum surface for interpretive interventions a selection of those elements in the material that may successfully illustrate for analysands that when they were speaking, they encountered a conflict over something being revealed, which caused them involuntarily and unknowingly to react in identifiable ways. [Gray 1986, p. 253]

While Gray's method is ideal for analyzing resistances, there are other components of resistance and ego analysis that remain to be explored. In short, we cannot equate resistance analysis with analysis of the ego, and it is too early to equate Gray's method of resistance analysis with all of resistance analysis even though its role as a model of analysis will remain an important one. For example, analysis of some resistances can effectively occur within the context of the ego's regressive states, using the method of free association. What is striking about free association is that its use as an objectified measure of what is going on in the patient's mind has only rarely been discussed. Given the various states of ego regression described in this book, if used as a source of data for helping patients see a picture of what is on their mind, free association becomes an extremely effective method for ego analysis. For example, a psychiatrist with a long history of difficulty with intimacy and a wish for closer relationships began a session by describing his increasing capacity to become close with a woman he had been dating for some time. This was then followed by a diatribe against analysis, especially its distancing elements. In this he brought up the "usual suspects" (the therapist's silence, not looking at the therapist, etc.). He then described seeing patients that morning, finding himself perplexed, and wondering how the therapist would deal with the material he was hearing. I could then point out how his descriptions of growing involvement with both a woman and me was sandwiched around his complaints about the distance in analysis. This suggested that those elements of analysis that could be experienced as distancing were called up by him to counteract his growing feelings of closeness, which indicated a need for him to have some distance. In this way we could see a defense in operation via his associative process. Thus, the complaint regarding the therapist's "distance" could be seen as a defense against the anxiety associated with closeness. In an associative sense, he was saying, "Thank goodness there is some distance here." What he consciously longed for, greater closeness, was most feared. In short, it is another route into the ego's operation, using the more objectified data of the patient's associations. It is not taking place outside of what the patient is capable of allowing into consciousness and, from that perspective, what is available to the conscious ego. Reminding the patient of what he or she has said with a comment like, "If we listen to what you have just said. . ." and then recounting associations, seems to make it easier for the patient to reflect on what was just said. This approach is presented to emphasize, as I have done throughout, that there are many issues to consider in our growing exploration of how to best utilize the ego in psychoanalytic treatment.

Gray's view of the ego as a passive observer in the face of conflict seems descriptively accurate:

> Analysands are not familiar with the nature of the activi-
> ties in which the mind-at-surface quietly engages while
> they are speaking. Indeed, they are barely even aware of
> the existence of these activities. For instance, the natural
> orientation of their thinking is restricted to regarding the
> things they say as references solely to what they have been
> talking about. [1986, p. 253]

There is a question as to whether this state of the ego is primarily due to the ego's need to be driven toward observation by conflict alone, as described by Gray. I would suggest that as part of any conflict, there is an *ego in regression,* and as this becomes resolved, higher-level ego functioning is brought to bear on the data of the analysis. This seems to fit the data of analysis in which one sees increasing ego-observing and integrating skills developing throughout a successful analysis, albeit with frequent regressions of various lengths. What one expects to see are increasingly higher levels of thought brought to bear on a problem, while changes in ego attitudes associated with less conflicted functioning also become more evident. These latter changes would be along the line of Emde's (1991) recent conclusions, based on neurophysiological, experimental, and developmental data, that from early on infants are exploratory and stimulus seeking. An attitude of curiosity and the capacity for surprise, which are both present from early in life, are aspects of ego functioning that become caught in conflict, and as one analyzes these conflicts, changes in ego attitudes do occur.

The notion of a more "active" ego as resistance analysis goes on is implied in Gray's written work. In referring to a paper by Rapaport, he states:

> It looks at an ego that is subject to the drive derivatives as
> being more passive than an ego that can "take charge,"
> which would be active (I am opting—I'm not sure Rapaport

did—for the latter activity as taking place in consciousness,
or at least available to awareness, i.e. more autonomous
than under the influence of unconscious fantasy). [Gray,
personal communication]

In this passage Gray suggests that, as the drive derivatives
become more conscious, one begins to see a more active,
"take charge" ego. This view of the ego has important
consequences for analysis of the more subtle, complicated
resistances. It further touches on the issue of the ego's
capacity to be interested in itself as an analysis goes on. This
then has implications for the reliance on close process monitoring throughout an analysis as the only way to bring the
resistances to consciousness. I believe we are only in the
rudimentary stages of understanding some of these changes
that occur in the ego and the techniques that best help these
to come about. I will attempt to outline some of these
changes, to contrast this perspective with Gray's more passive view of the ego.

Much of the work of analysis is geared toward ego
expansion. After we have explained the "basic rule" to the
patient and he or she has come upon the first resistance, we
are able to demonstrate a process of inhibition in action and
ultimately connect this to the symptom (although not in this
intellectualized fashion). Thus, our very first efforts are directed toward the main causes of ego inhibition—the resistances. In this and other ways, we begin to show our patients
that their thoughts and behavior have meaning. Some of the
most enlightening moments for patients occur when they can
see that what seemed like "idle" thoughts are really an
integrated series of thoughts with important personal significance or that the first time coming late to a session is a
statement and not a circumstance. At the same time we are
working with these aspects of the resistances to understanding thoughts and actions as meaning, we are analyzing
the threats that keep the resistances in place. From this we
can expect a gradual change in the feelings of safety associated with mental exploration, with the result being greater

conscious tolerance for thoughts. This greater sense of safety gives the patient the increasing ability to hold much more of what is going on in the session in consciousness.

Rather than observe a passive ego throughout the analysis, one would expect that as the analysis of the unconscious ego resistances went on, we would see an ego with greater autonomy and flexibility. It is at these times that patients seem capable, even temporarily, of more large-scale observations of their resistances. One can see an ego that is freer to judge and evaluate thoughts, and the therapist's observations of them, removed from the sense of threat accompanying similar observations. The patient who early in treatment gets angry at the suggestion that his bitter "thoughts" over his wife's unresponsiveness might have meaning for him can make the distinction later on between the fact that while his wife may very well be unresponsive at times, the fact that it is coming to his mind likely has more significance to *him*. Or the patient who feels attacked when her perception of the therapist's greeting as not particularly friendly is queried can wonder herself why she may have been so attuned to this nuance. Such is the fare of every therapist, and it bespeaks a patient's ego functioning with greater autonomy. As this occurs, we are dealing with an ego that has the capacity to deal with the more complicated and subtle resistances that are an integral part of the analytic process. Of course, casting one's interpretive net wide enough so that it captures the complexity of the patient's resistance, while staying close enough to what the patient is consciously capable of remembering, is a constant struggle for the therapist as he or she attempts to stay in empathic contact with the patient.

When we analyze resistances and associated threats, we are not only analyzing contents but also an ego in regression. When in the throes of a resistance, patients truly believe, unconsciously, that if they say what is on their mind, they will die, fragment, be left alone forever, be castrated, and so forth. In areas of conflict, the ego remains, at some bedrock level (and unconsciously), at the level of functioning when the conflict was in development. As Sandler (1975) so aptly puts it:

> [A]n organized unconscious world (or more precisely, a succession of unconscious worlds) continues to function outside of consciousness, according to childhood laws of cognition and perception; that childhood theories, beliefs, assumptions and premises *continue to operate* in the present, and that any new information or experience will, in the first instance, be apperceived and responded to according to the theories and structures of the persisting unconscious world. What persists is not only the *content* of past memories, fantasies, defenses, wishes, object relationships, instinctual urges and so on, but *also* schemata or structures representing organized modes of functioning, of making connections, conceptions of causality or temporal sequentiality, of anticipation and justice, of the absence of chance events, the egocentric cognitive viewpoint—all the things which Piaget has investigated and described. [p. 374]

When we begin to interpret the resistances, we not only interpret the content but also the form and structure of thinking that is part of the resistance and also unconscious. This is true not only in terms of the nature of the resistance (i.e., silence, the fear of silence, etc.) but also in relationship to the particular type of threat. Resistance analysis illuminates thinking characteristic of young children. Common examples of this are egocentric thinking (e.g., "My therapist looks tired. He must be bored with me.") and magical thinking (e.g., "If I say this I will be killed."). By bringing these ways of thinking to consciousness, we are beginning to expose them to higher-level ego functioning (Loewald 1971) and to elucidate how the patient's thinking represents "a rationalized version of more primitive thinking" (Sandler, 1975, p. 374). Much of the structure of the thinking in the resistances represents thought patterns from an earlier period of time. As these, along with the threats associated with them, are exposed to consciousness, we see a gradual movement to thinking characteristic of later phases of development.

As noted earlier, the patient in the throes of an intense resistance will think, and think about their thinking, in ways that are characteristic of what Piaget called preoperational thought, which occurs before age 7. Patients who show the most complex and subtle thinking when functioning well in their area of expertise respond consistently to only one of a range of possible stimuli when caught up in a resistance. The narcissistically vulnerable individual will most frequently be associating or not within a context of feeling unsupported or shamed, while the masochist's framework will entail some form of feeling pushed around by the therapist. The resistances will always be expressed in some form of action that is usually thought of as symbolic but is more likely to be an action signifier. The patient who leaves spaces between his thoughts so they do not touch or never leaves spaces so thoughts are always touching is expressing in action form signifiers of a resistance.

Flavell's (1963) contrasting of *action-based* thought with more *representational* thought serves as a clinical model for the patient's thinking while in a resistance versus when the resistance has been successfully analyzed over time.

> Piaget likens it to a slow-motion film which represents one static frame after another but can give no simultaneous and all-encompassing purview of all the frames. Representational thought, on the other hand, through its symbolic capacity has the potential for simultaneously grasping in a single, internal epitome, a whole sweep of separate events. It is a much faster and more mobile device which can recall the past, represent the present, and anticipate the future in one temporally brief, organized act. [p. 152]

Flavell describes other characteristics of representational thought, such as the capacity to reflect upon itself and its own organization and the ability to extend its vision beyond immediate concrete events and objects. Again, this is the type of thinking one sees developing over time as we continue to bring the resistances to consciousness. Thus, what we are dealing with during much of resistance analysis is an *immature ego*. This situation does not change our methods to be used (i.e., careful attention to the observable resistance in action) in that they are ideally suited to the immature ego that functions in a very concrete, static fashion. However, as the work goes on, we expect the patient to begin to think more representationally and thus become more open to observations that call on flexible and integrative thinking. We expect to see increasing evidence of more mature ego functioning, and as this develops, we can expect some changes in the patient's capacity to observe, think about, and grasp his or her own thought processes.

A patient's capacity to understand and integrate larger swatches of resistance material also depends on working with resistances to thinking and transference resistances. Such resistances as what it means to listen to the therapist, the reluctance to think integratively, and the reluctance to think like the therapist are examples of the types of resistances we are working on throughout the analysis that lead to greater tolerance to hear the therapist speak and greater freedom for the patient to think. For example, the patient who feels guilty when soothed by the therapist's voice cannot attend to the therapist for too long without becoming anxious. The man who equates his excitement over "finding his thoughts" with abandonment by his depressed, controlling mother can only tolerate the smallest of understanding before feeling threatened. The woman who experiences thinking like the therapist as being controlled by him cannot follow the therapist's thinking for too long without starting to feel uncomfortable. These are the types of resistances that make close process monitoring the preferable mode of resistance interpretation for the initial phase of the analysis, until aspects of the threat can be brought to awareness. Once the resistances have been worked on in this manner, we have windows into realms of thought that are more conflict-free, and the range of acceptable thoughts and thinking becomes wider. It is at these times we might expect the patient's capacity for integrative thought to be increased, thus leading them to be more open to the subtler shadings of the resistance that pervade the patient's thinking.

In addition to the liberation of certain ego *functions* during the analysis, one can also expect the reemergence of various ego *pleasures* that will also allow for more integrative functioning. Klein (1976) outlines some of these pleasures associated with ego activities as functioning (i.e., the activity itself is pleasurable), effectance (i.e., changing a course of action through one's behavior), and synthesis (i.e., establishing a sense of order and wholeness). These are similar to ego activities noted by Erikson (1963) and White (1963). During those times in the analysis when one or more of these pleasures is allowable to the patient, one sees greater receptivity to knowing, integrating, and doing more. If a patient is in a period of time when they can find pleasure in these functions, we can potentially have an inhibitory effect if we continue to interpret the resistances too narrowly.

I would agree with Gray's (1986) emphasis when he states, "I am interested in methodology for drawing more fully on the relatively autonomous capacities of analysands to strengthen both their motivation for and their work in analyzing" (pp. 245–246). However, these capacities do not just suddenly appear at the end of an analysis. One gradually sees these capacities develop over a period of time, which allows the patient to bring greater integrative and creative capacities to the work. There is not only the ability to function integratively that develops but the desire or press to function in this way. Such patients become interested in the connections between their thoughts, and they are thus more receptive to a wider source of material. The scope of their attention is not limited to the immediate resistance action pattern. Its antecedents within a session, between sessions, and historically may all be potentially integrated. This is not simply a progressive capacity but rather subject to wide fluctuations as conflict is activated and partially understood. However, to miss those times when the patient is receptive to more integrative functioning is to miss expanding conscious awareness of increasingly complex links among material and the subtle resistances to them.

My major point in this section is that throughout an analysis of resistances, we are not dealing with an ego of a single type. Our interpretations bring changes to the ego so that we see more mature levels of thinking, greater pleasures in thought processes, and a safer feeling in regard to a variety of thoughts. All of these allow for some flexibility in approaches to the resistances as the analysis progresses.

Finally, it is noteworthy that in analyzing certain unconscious ego defenses, we will not be working strictly within the drive derivative/defense paradigm. For example, in analyzing character resistances, we tend to work more with the temporary shifts *from* a defensive position. Thus, in determining when to intervene, we might need to wait for shifts from characteristic methods of associating like these: the laconic-appearing patient who rushes headlong from topic to topic, with an almost phobic reaction to lingering on a subject, who is reacting to an unconscious fear of being suffocated; the patient who always speaks in an even, well-modulated voice, with all traces of affect removed, thus unconsciously attempting to keep the therapist calm; or the patient who speaks very slowly, often pausing between different thoughts, and in this way unconsciously alleviating a "touching" fear. In these instances, it is the *temporary diminution of the conflict* that allows for the resistance to be pointed out. The shift is seen in the absence of a customary resistance. While still allowing the therapist to use the model of close process monitoring, it is not the usual method of analyzing the resistance as it is expressed in an emerging conflict.

THE ROLE OF THE SUPEREGO

With the introduction of Freud's (1926) second theory of anxiety, the understanding of the role of the threat to the ego in the resistances was clearly in place. However, as Gray

(1982) notes, Freud did not seem to hold fully to this view of the resistances even after 1926. Gray has returned to our awareness the concept of the centrality of the threat to the ego in resistances. After identifying that a resistance has occurred, understanding the threat to the ego becomes a key in reducing its effects on restrictions in thought processes. *Gray's view is that the primary threat to the ego is from a superego, reexternalized onto the therapist, which was experienced first from an earlier authority figure.* Thus, the threat is seen as coming from the therapist, who represents some aspect of a real or fantasized object relationship from the past. In fact, Gray (1987) sees resistance analysis as synonymous with superego analysis. "The essential characteristic lies in the strong emphasis on analysis of resistance, which is the central point of superego *analysis*" (p. 150). The technique of superego analysis is the technique of resistance analysis.

> By *analysis* of the superego, I mean: systematically making available to consciousness those repetitions of defensive formations in the analytic situation—including pre- and post-internalizations which were earlier mobilized, especially in connection with the oedipal situation, to the end that the compromised ego functions components can be progressively reclaimed, from the beginning of the analysis, by the relatively autonomous ego. [Gray 1987, p. 145]

While I agree with Gray that superego threats play an important part in many resistances, it seems to be *one of many threats* that can play a role in the central resistances that develop in most analyses. Furthermore, resistances seem to come from many levels of development and not only the oedipal phase.

I believe it useful to distinguish between resistances that develop *within* the ego stemming from a threat to the ego integrity and those that develop in response to a threat from a reexternalized object relationship. For example, there are those patients who become terrified with the arousal of depressive affect. For these individuals, whenever one of the inevitable pieces of mourning arises in their analysis, there is a frantic rush to action. This is most evident in those cases in which there has been an early loss, before the child is developmentally capable of mourning. The fear here is of an affect and the fantasy of its potentially disorganizing effects. The same is true for certain patients with the arousal of excitement. This is especially true in those patients when they have been overstimulated (e.g., by excessive parental nudity or aggression) or when there were deficiencies in the parental capacity to soothe the child at times of stress. Here again it is the arousal of an affect that brings on the fantasy of becoming overwhelmed, leading to a self-imposed inhibition as a calming device. The self psychologists have been especially helpful in broadening our understanding of the variety of threats that can arise within the ego, threatening its sense of integrity (see especially Kohut and Wolf 1978).

One patient frequently complained of feeling that she was "boring" and "uninteresting." The therapist did, in fact, find it hard to pay attention to her thoughts and often noticed his mind wandering to other issues. Half-formed thoughts that drifted into the air, delivered in a monotone, conveyed the impression there was nothing to pay attention to. Focusing on this particular voice led to thoughts of physical examinations by her physician-father through her adolescence and a period of bed-wetting while she was in latency, with the attendant feelings of extreme shame. Thus, it was a particular ego threat (loss of control and feelings of shame) that seemed to power the resistances in this situation.

I do not find internalizations, mobilized from the oedipal period, any more prominent in the resistances than internalizations from earlier and later phases. While obviously complicated to tease out as earlier conflicts become reworked in later phases, the resistances expressed in most analyses would seem to have roots in a variety of phases. Familiar to most therapists is the patient who leaves short pauses be tween thoughts, as an expression of a touching phobia from the anal phase. The patient who cannot take her thoughts too seriously, as a reflection of an earlier relationship with a depressed mother who could not be bothered with the demands of an active child, is another common reexternalization not strictly from the oedipal phase nor necessarily useful to think of this as a superego prohibition. Patients with controlling parents, especially during the adolescent years, will leave out of the analysis large sections of their lives as they attempt to protect their autonomy. For these patients full disclosure is a type of humiliating capitulation.

I have found it useful to keep a multicausal view of the resistances. Within any one resistance, there is the cause of this resistance at this particular moment in the analysis, while at the same time there are contributions from other sources at different developmental phases. A patient who sped through her sessions from the moment she rushed up the stairs to the time she jumped off the couch was reacting to the following threats: a fear of lingering anywhere too long, especially over her thoughts, as a reaction to wishes to play with her feces and accompanying prohibitions; an antidote to depressive affect that seemed humiliating and womanly; an expression of fantasized phallic power as a reaction to expected feelings of weakness and shame associated with being a woman; and a fantasy of being carried off to a quieter, less frantic (more womanly) way of being by her therapist–Prince Charming, but against her will and thus avoiding the wrath of the wicked stepmother. In all of these situations it is the specificity of the resistance and its particular developmental roots that seems capable of touching a responsive chord in the patient, while helping to bring the specific fear to consciousness. From this perspective, I find Gray's view of the centrality of the superego in resistances an important but restricted one, given our current state of knowledge. It is probably more useful to think of a *variety of disturbing signal affects* (Jacobson 1992), arising from fantasies based on conflicts stimulated by developmental interferences. It has also been suggested recently that resistances, rather than being the result of a reexternalized superego prohibition alone, are a creation of the therapist–patient pair that is unique to that particular analysis (Boesky 1992, Poland 1992).

DISCUSSION

More than any other therapist since Freud, Paul Gray has articulated a perspective on analyzing resistances that takes into account the structural theory and the second theory of anxiety. He has taken Freud's view of the resistances as something "which persists throughout the whole treatment and is renewed at every fresh piece of work" (Freud 1940, p. 178) and demonstrated what resistance analysis at the center of a psychoanalysis might look like. This perspective has been articulated from an ego-psychological point of view and has been a most convincing demonstration of its heuristic power.

While Gray's perspective on the analytic process is a welcome respite from the ritualistic symbolism or special empathic powers that can frequent clinical discussions of how the therapist came to intervene, much still needs to be explored. Thus, I would characterize his method in the following way. One listens for breaks or changes in voice in the patient's material. These are pointed out to the patient close to the time they are happening, since it is a time when the ego's functioning will be most observable to him. What will be driving these breaks are aggressive feelings turned upon the self, in response to a fear of the therapist's retaliation, which is a reflection of a reexternalized superego. By focusing in this limited way upon restrictions on allowing thoughts to come to mind, one will increase the patient's *"objective self-observing function"* (Gray 1990, p. 1093). This, in itself, will seemingly lead to the elaboration of the unconscious fantasies underlying the resistance.

As I have tried to indicate above, there are aspects of this view that may need to be expanded to fit in with clinical experience. These include the following:

1. While close process monitoring is an extremely useful technique throughout analysis, it may not be the only technique for bringing resistances to the patient's attention or working with them. We would expect areas of autonomous ego functioning to develop over the course of an analysis that would lead the patient to be capable of working with broader swatches of the resistance. What initially might be amenable to observation only by staying with the most immediate, surface observation of a resistance, at a later time in the analysis might be the beginning of a larger elaboration of a pattern of resistance and its possible causes. We would expect some gradual lessening of the threat over time so that what was unacceptable at an earlier time would not necessarily be so at a later time.

2. While retreating from aggressive thoughts in response to an anticipated negative response from the therapist (as a re-externalized superego) is a significant factor in forming resistances for many patients at some point in their analysis, clinical experience indicates it is not the *only* threat. *It is simply one threat among many,* which are as varied and subtle as the nature of the resistances themselves.

3. It has been my impression that the capacity for self-observation does *not* develop spontaneously as a by-product of the interpretation of the resistances. In fact, it seems more likely that the capacity for self-observation has its own set of resistances that can be different from those involved in obstructing the associative process. These resistances to self-observation play as significant role in the analysis as resistances to the associative process. Thus, a patient telling the therapist thoughts without restrictions but unable to linger over them for any length of time was enacting a toilet training fantasy of "emptying" his thoughts for the therapist, with the understanding that this would keep the therapist interested and involved. What was threatening was having independent thoughts or holding back, which was associated

with the therapist's disappearance. In such a situation, it was not the holding back of thoughts that was a problem, but rather doing something with those thoughts.

Gray has crystallized for all therapists the role of the threat in resistances. No therapist has paid such systematic attention to this aspect of resistances, providing a way out of the clinical morass that characterized previous writings on resistances (see my discussion of Greenson, Busch 1992). However, what is easy to lose sight of in Gray's work is that the subtlety of distinguishing between that which is threatened and that which is threatening—or, to put it another way, that which is resistance and that which is resisted against— is not always so easy to determine. Thus, a patient who reported all his dreams in a dry, intellectualized manner could be seen to be warding off involvement because of fears of being made into a woman, while at the same time expressing his disdain for the feminized therapist who believed in such ephemeral expressions of thoughts and feelings as dreams. Knowing when to highlight the lack of involvement as resistance versus hostility is the fodder of everyday analytic skill and insight. However, one can get the impression from Gray's work that a resistance is a resistance is a resistance. This is in contrast to the position of Apfelbaum and Gill (1989) "that what is defense at one moment in relationship to a given wish may in the next moment become the wish defended against" (p. 1076).

In fact, the whole role of id-driven unconscious fantasies in Gray's view of the analytic process, the need for their elucidation, and how he sees this occurring within the context of his method for observing resistances (i.e., close process monitoring) need further clarification. At times he gives the impression that if resistance analysis is successfully accomplished, the drive derivatives will arise (and be worked through?) spontaneously. For example, in commenting on the use of the power of the transference in overcoming resistances, Gray (1992) has said, "Such measures do a great deal for bringing id derivatives into consciousness, *but without allowing them to move forward naturally,* as they would if the analyst brought to life and made palpable the ego's specific incessant responses silently bent on resistance" (p.309, italics added). He has also stated that the drive derivatives need to be specified as part of any resistance analysis.

> Certainly it seems demonstrably true that consistent defense analysis that (*without neglecting reference to something identifiably being defended against*) is concerned with analyzing the *safety-seeking motives* for resisting drive derivatives, leads to greater access to formerly unconscious id *and* ego; but it does put the analyst eventually more on the receiving end. [Gray personal communication, italics in parentheses added]

In ending, let me remind the reader of what Lear (1990) said regarding the study of Freud: "If we are to treat psychoanalysis as a science and Freud as a scientist, we must not approach his texts as holy writ. What we have here is a first, brilliant attempt of humans to come to understand themselves in certain ways" (p. 17). What Gray has accomplished is to help us clearly see again, and in new ways, the unique role of resistances in psychoanalysis and to begin to chart a method for analyzing them. Only through continued questioning can we expand the boundaries of our clinical technique in dealing with this most subtle and elusive construction of the mind.

M. N. SEARL'S (1936) "SOME QUERIES ON PRINCIPLES OF TECHNIQUE"

Searl's (1936)[1] article is a brilliant exposition on the significance of resistance analysis, as well as a singular exploration of some technical variables to be considered when the role of the ego is contemplated as part of our interpretive methods. I consider it one of the pre-eminent examples in our literature of an ego-psychological approach to the psychoanalytic process.

Searl grasps the clinical implications of Freud's (1923, 1926) introduction of the structural theory and his second theory of anxiety as have few authors before or since. If my reading of the significance of the article is correct, it is deserving of further study because it is a remarkable historic document that presages the thinking of psychoanalytic

---

1. Throughout this chapter I will be referring to this same paper, so that the year will not be listed at each citation. Other Searl papers will be cited separately.

scholars writing in this same area some forty to fifty years later (A. Kris, Gray, Schafer 1983).

Searl's article also stands out as an exceptional rendering of the psychoanalytic process with the ego at the center of the analytic work. Like few papers in our field, it gives the clinician a feeling for an ego psychological approach to the data of psychoanalysis that is an alive, dynamic method of working in the clinical situation. Yet I have only seen Searl's paper referenced in two works, widely separated in time but not in tone (Fenichel 1941, Gray 1982). Its absence from the literature seems, in part, due to our long-standing struggle to integrate the structural theory with clinical technique (Apfelbaum and Gill 1989, Gray 1982).

Searl's paper compares favorably to well-known works written contemporaneously, such as Reich's (1933) "Character Analysis" and A. Freud's (1936) "Ego and the Mechanisms of Defense." While Reich was one of the first to grasp the significance of resistance analysis in analytic work, he was not as consistent as Searl in applying an understanding of the ego in resistance analysis. Furthermore, as Schafer (1983) points out, Reich lapsed into thinking of resistance analysis as a battleground, with the richly textured meanings of resistances reduced to a type of motiveless opposition that needed to be rooted out. Searl's paper seems a compendium to A. Freud's work, providing a sophisticated approach to resistance analysis with adults, while extending our understanding of the role of the ego in clinical psychoanalysis.

I believe that the article that should have led the way toward an exciting exploration of Freud's new understanding of the role of the ego in the psychoanalytic process instead remains ignored. In the spirit of attempting to revive interest in this overlooked gem, I will present a summary of Searl's major points. For the sake of expository simplicity, I have broken her article into two major areas: resistance analysis and the role of the ego. In the article itself, as in the analytic process, these two areas are not as neatly divided.

ANALYSIS OF THE RESISTANCES

Searl's beginning assumption was that to that point (1936), Freud's views on resistance analysis were only a "promising way to pursue" (p. 471), not a detailed presentation of principles of technique. The implication was that much more needed to be explored about this new method of understanding resistances based upon Freud's second theory of anxiety. This refreshingly blunt appraisal of psychoanalytic understanding of resistance analysis stands in marked contrast to the more typical idealization through the years of Freud's contribution to the *clinical* methods of resistance analysis and our understanding based upon his contributions. It was almost fifty years later that Gray (1982) highlighted the developmental lag between psychotherapists' belief in the significance of resistance analysis and the level of sophistication of clinical thinking based upon our understanding of the ego's role in the formation of resistances.

While Freud's clinical brilliance led him to understand the crucial significance of resistance analysis, he never fully integrated the clinical potential of working with resistances from the perspective of the ego as the seat of anxiety. Searl was thus one of the first to highlight that while Freud's new views on resistances were promising, much needed to be learned. This seemed to allow her to pursue the technical implications of the theory, while her contemporaries and most of those who followed were in adulation of what was understood and thus kept repeating Freud's tendency to view the resistances as primarily something to overcome more than understand.

Searl approaches the specifics of resistance analysis from a number of subtly different but interlocking perspectives that not only are forerunners of current thinking but show a dazzling understanding of the complexities of the topic. She offers a clinical perspective that is timely and modern. Her clear descriptions of the technique and underlying assumptions of resistance analysis, presented via a series of observations and questions, gives the therapist a point of view from which to approach the resistances that is rare in the clinical literature even today.

> In the first place I find something to regret in the technical term "resistance," even though it may on the whole be the best shorthand for the purpose. It puts the emphasis on the negative strength exerted by the patient rather than on the cause. Analysis depends for its success on co-operation with that part of the patient's mind which, however mistakenly and ineffectively, seeks a better solution. In that sense, then, what we call analysis of resistance is really an analysis of ineffectual capacities, or of conflicting and mutually damaging processes. If we centre our activities as analysts on the aim of restoring his full capacities to the patient, we are constantly asking ourselves such questions as "Why can he not . . .?" "Why is there a difficulty?"' Then we are able to limit our activities to explaining those difficulties when and as we see them. [p. 481]

> This method Freud contrasts with "divining from the patient's free associations what he failed to remember." We cannot therefore doubt that Freud wished to substitute interpretation of resistance for interpretation of absent content.
> The analysis of resistance seems to me, then, to imply the knowledge of "what" is subservient to the understanding of "why?" or "why not?"', and close adherence to this simplifying principle can alone gradually bring clarity and order into confusing varieties of attempts to deal with the patient's material, and can ultimately give us a firm basis from which to proceed. [pp. 476–478]

> If on the other hand, we say to a patient, "You are thinking so and so," "You have had such and such a phantasy," and so on, we give him no help about his inability to know that for himself, and leave him to some extent dependent on the analyst for all such knowledge. If we add "The nature of this thought or phantasy explains your difficulty in knowing for yourself," we still leave the patient with

increased understanding related to a particular type of thought and phantasy only, and imply, "One must know the thought or phantasy first before one can understand the difficulty about knowing about it." The dynamics of the patient's disability to find his own way have been comparatively untouched if the resistance was more than the thinnest of crusts, and will therefore still be at work to some extent and in some form whatever the change brought about by the interpretation of absent content. [pp. 478–479]

There are few places in the analytic literature one will find such a clear, straightforward description, free of jargon, that captures the essence of working with the resistances and its underlying hypotheses, that is consistent with the structural theory. Resistances are presented as adaptations from an earlier time that have gone awry and are now interfering with the individual's functioning (i.e., ineffectual capacities). Searl's central question in approaching the resistances—"*What* is being resisted?"—keeps the therapist focused on the threat driving the resistance rather than circumventing it to get to the underlying fantasies (i.e., absent content) and overcome the resistance. Finally, her purpose is to help the patient find his or her own way by understanding what is impeding progress, rather than goals often associated with more authoritarian approaches to analysis (i.e., finding the buried memories, making the unconscious conscious, etc.).

Thus, Searl captures the essence of Freud's changed views of anxiety from being caused by a dammed-up libido to being the result of a threat to the ego. Translated into clinical terms, in the face of a resistance it is incumbent upon the therapist to consider the question of what threat the patient senses to avoid knowing more about his or her thoughts. If a resistance is in operation, it indicates that the patient is under some threat. The purpose of the resistance is to keep the threat from awareness. Interventions that do not respect the patient's resistance to certain thoughts and feelings becoming conscious will be irrelevant at best, and potentially dangerous.[2]

Resistance analysis is a free association–based, process-oriented approach that has come to be specifically championed in the literature only many years later. By focusing on the patient's relationship to his or her own thoughts, resistance analysis becomes the centerpiece of the analytic process based upon looking at what stops the patient from becoming aware of what is on his or her mind. This allows Searl to eschew combat metaphors that are so prominent in discussions of resistance technique through the years and that still serve as a point of attack for those arguing against what they view as "classical" technique of resistance analysis. Searl speaks to this point when she states:

> It is not, it seems to me, a method of "breaking" or of "conquering" or "melting" resistances or even of [showing] how "unreasonable" they are—although it is true that the patient's own recognition of some lack of reason in them is an essential preliminary to the desire for something better. *It is simply a method of understanding them.* [pp. 485–486, italics added).

The depth of Searl's understanding is captured in her discussion of resistance analysis versus the interpretation of what she calls "absent content." The essence of her position is that when the patient comes to some blockage in his thoughts, the question of *what* is being blocked is subservient to *why* there is a blockage.[3] The thoughts, fantasies, or

---

2. I realize I am simplifying the clinical process where "what is defense one moment in relation to a given wish may the next moment become the wish defended against" (Apfelbaum and Gill 1989). It is the heart of the complexity of the clinical process to know when to emphasize one aspect of the resistance over another. However, it has been the defense components of resistance analysis that have been neglected, and these may be usefully focused on in isolation both clinically and pedagogically.

3. While the resistances may take the form of an actual blockage of thoughts, there are an infinite number of ways the patient may keep himself from knowing or revealing thoughts while verbalization continues.

feelings being blocked or causing the block *may be* less significant than the specific threat the patient feels under at the time. As I have pointed out frequently in these chapters, even therapists who point to Freud's second theory of anxiety as a turning point in resistance analysis frequently fall into searching for the hidden unconscious fantasy or getting out the strangulated affect as primary methods of dealing with resistances. A frequently heard scenario in clinical discussions is one in which the patient's hesitation in talking is interpreted as being due to some feeling toward the therapist, before the question of the patient's reluctance is ever taken up. Schafer (1983) succinctly captures this same point, almost fifty years later:

> There are many moments in the course of an analysis when analysands seem to dangle *unexpressed content* before the analyst. These are the moments when the analyst is tempted to say, for example, "You are angry," "You are excited," or "You are shamed." But if it is so obvious, why isn't the analysand simply saying so or showing unmistakenly that it is so? To begin with, it is the hesitation, the obstructing, the resisting that counts. If the analyst bypasses this difficulty with a direct question or confrontation, the analysand is too likely to feel seduced, violated, or otherwise coerced by the analyst who has in fact, even unwittingly, taken sides unempathically. [(p. 75, italics added]

Searl sums up the contrast between the analysis of absent content and resistance analysis in the following manner:

> [T]he analysis of absent content says in effect: "We can conclude from what you have said that you are resisting such and such an affect, memory, thought or phantasy; and in order to know *why* you are resisting we have to first know *what* you are resisting"; the analysis of resistances says in effect, . . . "We can conclude from what you have said that you have taken and are taking such and such a

method of dealing with a painful situation. That way may have been the best you could find in some circumstances, but it contained an alteration of a real state of affairs to suit emotional troubles, and therefore, whatever it did for you, it had to leave some of the real difficulty not really dealt with. That is the difficulty you are meeting at the present time, and it is increasing any other difficulty you may have in keeping to the conditions of analytic treatment." [pp. 489–490]

In this view Searl also anticipates Stone's (1973) observation that resistances have an effective, functional, protective side that results from an adaptation to a situation perceived as overwhelming at one time. Thus, Searl defines a resistance as, "the best form of defense he has been able to adapt to a particular difficulty" (p. 480). She sees this as a crucial part in helping patients understand the logic for a resistance continuing in spite of the obvious difficulties it is causing, and thus Searl offers the patient the "fact that we recognize his difficulty and that we can offer a reason not only for it, but for his incapacity to emerge from it" (p. 478). It is a clinically useful perspective that can help with the accusatory/guilt components that creep into interpretations of resistance, while also making the patient's behavior perfectly understandable based on a solution to an earlier threat.

Clinical *bons mots* on the resistances exist throughout Searl's paper. The resistance as a joint creation of therapist and patient (p. 488, à la Boesky 1990); process-based resistance analysis as an antidote to the problem of "dosing" interpretations (p. 480); ways of dealing with conscious and intellectual resistances (p. 490)—these are just some of the clinically useful topics woven throughout Searl's larger discussion of the ego-psychological perspective on the resistances.

THE SIGNIFICANCE OF THE EGO
IN CLINICAL TECHNIQUE

If the context of Apfelbaum and Gill's (1989) conclusion that the technical implications of the structural theory seem not to have been noted and implemented, it is startling to find in Searl's paper so many issues germane to the clinical application of the ego in psychoanalysis. She offers an ego-based view of the analytic process that is a remarkable forerunner of current thinking while conveying, like few articles before or since, what this method of treatment looks like. She also formulates some goals for treatment with the ego at center stage that are models of clarity and reappear in our literature some fifty years later. Consider the following passage.

> Another pronounced advantage in the analysis of resistances is that it removes from the analyst the difficult and precarious business of "dosing" in determining the amount of anxiety to be aroused. That is left to the working of the patient's own mind in conjunction with circumstances extraneous to the analysis itself, and the test of the amount of anxiety he can bear is—for adult patients—the amount of anxiety-laden thought he has been able to put into words. A correct interpretation about the *reason why* he has not been able to put more into words still leaves the option with him. But to put his thought or feelings into words *for* him is to interfere with the action of a kind of mental sieve, depriving both the analyst of a sure guide about the integrating power of the ego, and the patient of the best form of defense he has been able to adapt to a particular difficulty; it is therefore one that should be left to him until he has found a better method. By telling him what he has not put into words, whatever the subsequent result, one has not increased but has rather provided a substitute for his own power of verbal expression in the particular instance under consideration. One is saying to him in effect "You see what your sieve was keeping back— how harmless, indeed how helpful this piece of knowledge, how unnecessary such rigid sieving," and one may indeed do much for the patient by such methods. But in addition to its use as an anxiety mechanism the process of discriminatingly sieving his thought may be very useful to him in other circumstances, and we do not want to injure it. In other words, one wants to further a power of reasonable choice and control rather than rigid censorship or lack of control between conscious thought and speech as well as between the conscious and the pre-conscious, and the

pre-conscious and the unconscious. And the quickest and surest way to this end is to [show] good reason, however misapplied, for its previous use rather than unreason. [pp. 480–481]

In this we see, again, Searl's view of the ego as the seat of anxiety, which allows in thoughts based on adaptations that were necessary at one time. She highlights the importance of not circumventing the ego's adaptations, primarily because she views ego strengthening via greater inclusion of the ego in the process of analysis as crucial to its success. Searl's premise, not generally accepted at the time and only recently a part of our understanding of the analytic process, is that what seems to happen in successful analyses is not the cessation of conflict but rather the ability to engage in a process of self-analysis when conflicts arise. Her views on this come close to those of outcome studies done many years later (Pfeffer 1961, Schlessinger and Robbins 1983). "The only satisfactory objective criterion of a finished analysis . . . involves the capacity to retain or quickly regain that total improvement, when tested by the independent facing of difficulties subsequently encountered"(Searl, p. 472). Compare this with Schlessinger and Robbins's conclusions that "[t]he effect of analysis is not the obliteration of conflict, but a change in the potential for coping with conflict" (p. 167).

From this premise follows one of Searl's major technical points: a significant component of any analysis needs to focus on those characteristic methods and conflicts that keep the patient from knowing more about him- or herself. Thus, if one believes that what analysis can provide, in part, is a way of understanding that helps the patient deal in an ongoing way with the the emergence of conflicts, then working on the barriers to that understanding needs to become a major part of the analytic task. As stated by Searl, "[T]hat which is important is not the extent to which *we* may be able to impart to the patient our knowledge of his life and psyche, *but it is the extent to which we can clear the patient's own way to it and give him freedom of access to his own mind*" (p. 487, italics added).

It is striking to compare this view with Gray's (1982) work in which he concludes that the results of analysis are dependent on the degree to which the patient's ego has been included as part of the process. In this point of view, the analytic task is framed as an attempt to give the patient greater mastery over and accessibility to his or her own thought processes. It is a process-oriented method that suggests patients use characteristic methods to keep themselves from knowing what they think, and knowing what they think about their thinking, as a way of warding off painful affects. Searl's perspective is to help the patient with those characteristic methods that prevent using the full range of ego capacities that are caught up in repressive and regressive measures. Over and over again she makes the point that her perspective is "What keeps the patient from saying?" or "What keeps the patient from knowing?" "By telling him what he has not put into words, whatever the subsequent result, one has not increased but rather has provided a substitute for his own power of verbal expression in the particular instance under consideration" (p. 480). Her approach is a forerunner of recent interest in the issue of self-analysis and anticipates Calef's (1982) remark that the results of analysis are related to the degree to which the patient has identified with the process. In Searl's work, the process of analysis is the focus, with the end result geared toward understanding those resistances toward self-analysis.

Searl also touches directly on an issue that therapists since Freud have struggled with—that is, what one does with the data of analysis (the patient's free associations). Once again, Searl's emphasis is remarkably prescient when compared with recent psychoanalytic authors (Gray, Davison et al. 1990, Levy and Inderbitzin 1990, Paniagua 1985, 1991) who suggest accrued analytic benefits by staying closely attuned to the surface of the patient's thoughts. This is in contrast to those who would look to the patient's thoughts unfailingly as symbolic representations of deeper unconscious meaning. Thus, with the first perspective a pause in the patient's associations might be pointed to as a resistance in operation, while the "depth" perspective might listen for the associations (the patient's or the therapist's) to determine what primitive instinctual impulse was being gratified. In essence, Searl's position is that there are numerous benefits to be gained by staying close to the surface of what the patient is saying.

> I believe that only when one abandons the attempt to deal directly with absent content and with truly unconscious material—or at least when one tries to do so—does one become aware of the wider possibilities of analytic work which lie hidden in the conscious and preconscious material—the re-grouping, the re-arrangement of it, the dissolving of compulsive fusions, the tracing of hidden links, unsuspected connections, etc. This work of putting things in places to which they belong, making true wholes and separating false ones, can be more effectively carried out, I believe, if the analyst keeps his own work to which the patient allows that it belongs—voluntarily expressed material. It can hardly be necessary to say that one does not abandon one's knowledge of the "true unconscious" because one makes no attempt to apply it directly. All that is in question is the best way in which the patient himself may reach such knowledge. [p. 484]

Here Searl is making the point that there are many components of what might be called the observable data between therapist and patient that is the basis of useful analytic data. When compared to some of Gray's recent comments, one can see again how forward looking Searl's views were.

> In listening to the patient, I focus on the flow of material with an ear for evidence, at the manifest surface level. [1990, p. 1085]

> My aim is a consistent approach to *all* of the patient's words, with priority given to what is going on with and within those productions as they make their appearance, not with attempts to theorize about what was in mind at some other time and place. [1992, p. 324]

Compare this with a recent conjecture reported by Joseph (1988). After Joseph made an interpretation, the patient fell silent, then reported some good work he had recently accomplished. "Instead of my patient becoming aware that I had opened up something useful and feeling anything about it, he introjected this useful object/analyst and, using projective identification, forced the listening valuing part of his own self into me, then split up and projected the people listening to him and praising him" (pp. 632–633).

Searl points out that deep interpretations of absent content enforce a type of passivity on the patient. It also encourages a belief in the therapist's omniscience, while stimulating the patient's omnipotent fantasies and encouraging magical thinking. Freud himself struggled with this issue, and it was not unusual for there to be within the same paper (see Freud 1910a) a critique of not staying close to what the patient was talking about and could be aware of, and the suggestion that this could do no harm and possibly do some good. It was a consequence, at times, of the struggle between Freud the clinician and Freud the theoretician and, at other times between competing models of the mind (e.g., anxiety resulting from a dammed-up libido versus the ego's response to threat). Searl's work is consistent and current with the newer approaches to the clinical application of ego psychology.

Finally, Searl's paper is filled with sensible clinical guidelines based on a solid understanding of the ego's role in the defensive process. As an example, her observations on the role of action seem positively brilliant and could serve as a useful reminder in any discussion of the topic.

> Naturally the analyst, like the patient, learns much from the action, bearing and expression of the other; but, for the analyst's purposes, the knowledge thus gained is and remains secondary to that from verbal expression, in the sense (1) that his interpretations should be based on and referable to or explicable in terms of what the patient has put into words and that alone; and (2) that our chief concern is with that which prevents him putting more into words. We are taking away the patient's accepted and

reasonable responsibility if we in any way shift the importance away from the only, though the very difficult, technique which analysis asks of him; and we encourage belief
in magic, which is independent of conditions, if we do not
evince our belief in the conditions in which analysis can be
carried on. How to be firm about it without being harsh or
rigid is indeed a problem for the analyst, but an essential
one. [p. 489]

Here again we see Searl focusing on the action as a
possible resistance that needs to be explored. This is in
contrast to much of the other literature on action, beginning
with Deutsch (1952), in which action is seen as just another
form of communication or an impediment to progress, and
interpretations seem directed not to the reasons for the
resistance occurring in action form but to a determination of
the symbolic meaning of the behavior as an attempt to break
a treatment impasse (e.g., see Anthi 1983). In this we can see
the return to a battleground metaphor à la Reich, in which
the action as an unconscious ego resistance is seen as as
impediment rather than an inherent aspect of the treatment.
Searl focuses on the form of the behavior. She asks what to
me seems the most germane question: why is the behavior
occurring in this particular form? This leads her to wonder
what use can be made of actions and what the consequences
are of doing so. I have found it more clinically useful to think
of action as Searl does—as being a manifestation of a behavior occurring in a regressed form that is not easily usable
by the patient (Busch 1989, 1993).

In discussing action, Searl again raises the problem
caused for the patient by interpreting without his or her
participation. In addition to what she has already pointed out
(i.e., it encourages a belief in magical thinking and the
omniscience of the therapist, and it puts the patient in a
passive position), Searl suggests that using this method
discourages the patient's increasing participation in the analytic process. This perspective (i.e., the role of the ego in the
interpretive process), along with Searl's other major contribution in this paper (i.e., a clinical approach from the side of

the resistances), could fruitfully have been one direction that investigations of the ego in the psychoanalytic process went after Freud's initial formulations. That the article was instead neglected was a loss to psychoanalysis that only recently has begun to be corrected.

POSTSCRIPT

Who was M. N. Searl, and why was her article ignored? I can offer the reader some data, some speculations, and some intriguing questions. In short, I would like to offer the possibility that what happened to Searl and her article seems to represent one of the more bizarre and tragic examples of our difficulty in integrating the structural model into our psychoanalytic theory of treatment. If, as indicated above, this is not a problem only from the past, it should prove to be a useful chapter to future historians on the politics of theory.

M. N. (Nina) Searl, a training analyst at the British Psycho-Analytic Institute, was a significant contributor to the psychoanalytic literature from 1924 to 1938. According to Mosher's (1991) *Index to Psychoanalytic Journals*, she published fourteen articles during this time, all in the *International Journal of Psycho-Analysis*. From the archives of the British Psycho-Analytic Society, I have also learned that from 1924 to 1937 she was a frequent presenter at their scientific meetings (eighteen presentations during this time). In addition to being a prolific writer, she was one of the first (if not the first) to present a paper to the British Psycho-Analytic Society on the technique of child psychoanalysis. However, her psychoanalytic career ended abruptly in 1937, just one year after the publication of "Some Queries on Principles of Technique."

In King and Steiner's (1991) comprehensive account of the Freud–Klein controversies in the British Psycho-Analytic Society, we learn that Searl was a long-standing target of a Kleinian vendetta. In the second in a series of meetings held between February and June 1942 to discuss the acrimony

and distrust between the Freudians and Kleinians, Dr. Me-
litta Schmidberg, who was Melanie Klein's daughter and one
of her fiercest critics, scathingly attacked the Kleinians for
trying "to force their opinions on us, and to browbeat us by
subtle and by not so subtle methods into accepting it" (King
and Steiner 1991, pp. 97–98). In this context, Schmidberg
had the following to say about Searl:

> About 1932 started the crusade against Miss Searl. To give
> only one example of the methods employed: when she gave
> lectures for candidates Kleinian training analysts and full
> Members attended them in order to attack her concertedly
> in the subsequent discussion in front of the candidates.
> This induced the Training Committee to lay down the rule
> that Members should not attend lectures for candidates. In
> the meetings no occasion was omitted to make a joint
> attack on her.
> After the attack against Miss Searl was brought to a
> successful conclusion, the methods worked out were em-
> ployed on others. [King and Steiner 1991, p. 93]

The "successful conclusion" Schmidberg refers to was that
in November 1937, Searl resigned from the society. It is
important to note that no member disputed Schmidberg's
facts and that the attacks on Searl led to the aforementioned
changes by the training committee.

Why this Kleinian cabal against Searl? What we do know
is that individuals go on the attack when feeling threatened.
I am particularly intrigued with the possibility that Searl's
work on the ego was a threat to the Kleinians' characteristic
ways of thinking about the analytic work. I have seen similar
(although certainly more subdued) responses to Gray's work,
where his focus on the technical implications of Freud's ego
psychology and the unconscious resistances is either mistakenly taken by some as a repudiation of the role of unconscious fantasies in mental life or (possibly even more
hostilely) dismissed as already well known. A. Freud (1965)
notes the hostility I am describing and puts it in a historical
perspective.

In the earliest era of psychoanalytic work . . . there was a marked tendency to keep the relations between analysis and surface observations wholly negative and hostile. This was the time of the discovery of the unconscious mind and of the gradual evolvement of the analytic method, two directions of work which were inextricably bound up with each other. It was then the task of the analytic pioneers to stress the difference between observable and hidden impulses rather than the similarities between them and, more important than that, to establish the fact in the first instance that there existed such hidden, i.e., unconscious motivation. [p. 32]

Searl's work emphasized not only the benefits but also the necessity of staying closer to the surface at times—to observe and work with the resistances and to encourage the process of self-analysis. This was anathema to those therapists who defined the analytic task as the "sole concentration on the hidden depth of the mind" (A. Freud 1965, p. 32). There have been other suggestions as to why there has been this difficulty in integrating an ego-psychological perspective with clinical technique (Busch 1992, 1993, Gray 1982), but I do not believe we have penetrated to the reasons for the degree of antagonism as seen in the attacks on Searl and the unpleasantness of the Freud-Klein controversies.

In relation to "Some Queries on Principles of Technique," it seems clear that at the time of its publication Searl was caught in the psychoanalytic maelstrom sweeping through the British Psycho-Analytic Society, which likely affected the hearing this paper got at the time. Also potentially contributing to this was Searl's withdrawal from psychoanalysis and the tragic circumstances surrounding it.[4]

---

4. Scott (personal communication) reports on the meeting in which Searl resigned.

As I remember it (and I know many other people's memories are very different and I have never discovered what was in the minutes of that meeting) she said she wished to make a personal statement. She said that she had begun to hear the voices of her

I hope this review of the paper will go some way to restoring it to a significant place in the psychoanalytic literature. It is significant that this is Searl's *second* "neglected classic" (Scott 1976). While this other article is of a very different type, I know of no other psychoanalytic author with this dubious honor. Whether Searl's epiphany is part of a larger corpus deserving of study is another question worthy of further investigation.

---

hallucinating patient and knew that this was not analysis and that she must resign in order to discover what was going on in her life. I do not remember discussing details after the meeting with anyone, and the next I heard was years later when I heard she had become a fire warden in London during the war. And much later I heard that her life ended as a nun or at least as a resident in a convent.

RESISTANCE ANALYSIS AND OBJECT RELATIONS THEORY

While it is difficult to make generalizations regarding the numerous theories considered under the heading of object relations, certain recent trends emerge in relationship to the resistances. Succinctly put, these theories usually *misunderstand* the resistances in what they refer to as "classical analysis." Where offered, object relations theories of resistances seem designed to overcome resistances via parameters or interpretations within an objects relations perspective. Respect for and careful investigation of the resistances as a necessary component of the analytic process seem not to be an integral part of these theories.

For example, in Greenberg and Mitchell's (1983) study of object relations theory and its relationship to "other" psychoanalytic theories, resistance is lumped together with Freud's pre-1915 views of *repression* in a section called "Resistances and Repression." Resistance as a separate clinical entity is not described. It is as if they were saying the classical view of resistance is the same as Freud's pre-1915 view of repression (it is not), while ignoring Freud's designation of the resistances as an entity arising in the action of the psychoanalytic situation. Within this context it is ironic that object relations theorists have brought certain key experiences to the attention of therapists that have enriched our understanding of resistances and allowed for a greater range of more finely textured understanding. However, psychotherapists have always struggled with translations of empathic understanding into usable analytic communications, and this issue remains a central problem in analytic technique.

Object relations theorists are not alone in their misunderstanding of the "classical" technique of resistance analysis. As noted previously, there has been what Gray (1982) calls a developmental lag in our understanding of the resistances. Gray also highlights Freud's ambivalence toward changing his technical approach to the resistances, even with his increasing knowledge about them. Furthermore, as I have suggested elsewhere in this book, it was only with the introduction of Freud's second theory of anxiety within the structural model (Freud 1923, 1926) that a true psychoanalytic understanding of how to analyze the resistances could emerge. Before this, the anxiety leading to the resistances was seen as a by-product of dammed-up libido. Therefore, the goal was to free the libido by bringing unconscious wishes into consciousness. The resistances, at this time, were seen as a barrier to be overcome. After they were brought into consciousness, the psychotherapist was called on to use various methods (e.g., promises of rewards of health, use of the positive transference, suggestion) to help the patient push on in the face of resistances.

As we shall see, this earlier view of resistance analysis is the one object relations theorists present as the current "classical view" of resistance analysis, which they then go on to attack. However, in Freud's second theory of anxiety, the ego was seen as the source of anxiety. That is, anxiety was seen to occur when the ego perceived a danger (i.e., where it feared being overwhelmed), which was further seen as a repetition of an earlier traumatic situation. The resistances were now seen as the ego's response to anxiety. With this conceptual understanding of the underlying psychic mechanism in place, psychotherapists could then grasp the full meaning of the resistances as the result of a perceived danger to the ego. Differences among clinical techniques of resistance analysis depend, in part, on how closely the therapist follows the view of the "ego as the sole seat of anxiety" (Freud 1926, p. 161).[1]

As an example of the confusion on the "classical" psychoanalytic technique of resistances seen in one object relations theorist, let us turn to a sampling of Mitchell's (1988) views on the subject.

> The analyst, whose function is to investigate and uncover, is pitted against the resistances, whose function is to protect and keep hidden the infantile wishes and longings. The ultimate aim of psychoanalysis is to overcome the resistance, to flush out the beast, to "track down the libido . . . withdrawn into its hiding place" (Freud, 1912), to tame the infantile wishes by uncovering them through memory. . . .
>
> The analysand is encouraged to relax the defenses, to allow the derivatives of his wishful impulses to appear uncensored in his free associations. The analyst's function is to cull the infantile wishes and fears from the complexly disguised derivatives in which they are encased. . . .
>
> The resistance represents the manifestation of the original defense in this new, highly dangerous situation in which the repressed is being evoked. Wishful, bestial impulses were repressed originally because they posed a grave threat to the peacekeeping purposes of the ego; the analysis itself in its attempt to uncover the libidinal impulses through the analyst's interpretations, poses a similar grave threat. [pp.281–282]

---

1. Although many differences exist among those classified as object relations theorists, there is a similarity among them as to how they view the arousal of resistances in the analytic situation, and how they conceive of the therapist's task in dealing with the resistances, that sharply distinguishes them from contemporary ego psychologists. From this one perspective, talking of them as "object relations theorists" seems apt.

Mitchell's descriptions are indeed an accurate portrayal of Freud's views on resistance analysis, *but it is based on his pre-1926 formulations of the resistances in which anxiety is seen as the result of dammed up-libido.* Within this view, it is an analytic imperative to "flush out the beast" and uncover the hiding places of the infantile wishes as representatives of the libido. The resistances were seen as an obstacle to overcome via suggestion, influence, and interpretation from above (Freud 1914, 1917a,b,c). However, by the 1930s therapists were beginning to understand the technical implications of Freud's second theory of anxiety. This was evident in the work of Reich (1933) and A. Freud (1936) and succinctly elaborated in Searl's (1936) paper. Searl approached the resistances as adaptive responses that attempt to manage frightening emotions. She suggested that once a resistance was recognized, it was not enough to help the patient overcome it with educative measures. She stressed the importance of understanding the reasons for its formation and the patient's difficulty in emerging from it. Thus, Searl highlighted the significance of analyzing the fears and dangers that led to the formation of the resistances as the centerpiece of resistance analysis. She also pointed to the hazards of bypassing resistance analysis to unearth the unconscious derivatives. This is the classical technique of resistance analysis as underscored by current theorists such as Gray, Schafer (1983), and me. It is captured in Gray's pithy statement that "*the therapeutic results of analytic treatment are lasting in proportion to the extent to which during the analysis the patient's unbypassed ego functions have become involved in a consciously and increasingly voluntary co-partnership with the analyst*" (1982, p. 264).

A SENSE OF THE RESISTANCES: AN OBJECT RELATIONS PERSPECTIVE

I have used this heading because it is difficult to get a clear view of the resistances among some recent object relations theorists. For example, in Mitchell's (1988) book there is a one-page reference to resistances in the index, and this page is the aforementioned description of "problems" with the classical view. However, his description of the analytic process may give us some insight into how he might treat resistances.

Mitchell's (1988) view of the analytic situation is one in which the patient attempts to connect with split-off aspects of the self, while the relationship with the therapist is dominated by old anxieties and disappointments. "The analyst's dogged inquiry into anxiety-ridden areas of the patient's life, and his participation in new forms of interaction, enables the patient to encounter, name, and appreciate facets of his experience unknown before" (p. 289). Describing inquiry into areas the patient is anxious about as "dogged" (i.e., willful, stubborn) is an ominous sign. If one believes that anxiety is the result of a threat and that the resistances are adaptations based on old fears, then to do anything else except treat the anxiety and the resistances surrounding them with great respect seems, at best, a fruitless task. Also inherent within Mitchell's model is an idealization of the therapist and the new role he or she serves for the patient.

The subtle subtext of this model is that it is the therapist, rather than the patient, who is the catalyst for change. It is the therapist's method of interacting that brings about self-discovery, rather than the exploration of the patient's resistances to self-discovery. In this view it is the *activity* of the therapist that is the stimulus for change, while in the classical model it is the analysis of the patient's *resistances* to activity that is the model for change.

As it did for Winnicott (1965) and Balint (1950), the role of the patient's safety in the analytic situation plays a prominent role in the work of Modell (1988) and Greenberg (1991). In these theories the locus of the patient's anxiety changes from the intrapsychic to the interpersonal, with a sense of safety dependent on the personal influence of the therapist. From a broad position, one cannot disagree with the assertion that the therapist who does not help the patient manage anxiety in the analytic situation will have a deleterious effect on the patient's capacities for analytic work. However, it does not seem useful to look to the therapist's countertransference as the *exclusive* cause of the patient's unsafe feelings. Modell (1988), for example, sees the patient as setting up tests for the therapist by re-creating past traumas to see whether the therapist will repeat or disconfirm them. "If the analyst passes the patient's test, the analytic setting and the person of the analyst will be invested either consciously or unconsciously with attributes of a protective object" (p. 593). Within such a perspective, the classical view based on internal dangers occurring within the here and now of the transference recedes further into the background.

It is not that I see Modell's view as incorrect but rather one-sided. Under the guise of a new discovery, certain authors seem willing to give up one of Freud's great discoveries (i.e., our capacity to create, on the basis of complex compromise formations, a prism through which we view all interactions and thus make them all seem the same). Such views are not always based on the enactments of others. In short, every moment a patient feels unsafe cannot be placed solely on the therapist's inability to create a safe-enough situation. To counter such a bias, we need only think of those patients in whom the therapist's *interest in their safety makes them feel unsafe.* While a sense of safety in exploring one's thoughts is a highly desirable analytic goal, there are many points along the way where such a goal is frightening to the patient. In such situations, analysis geared only toward the therapist rather than the patient would be misguided.

Gray (1991) has argued that while the importance of creating a sense of safety may be necessary for certain wider-scope patients, its wholesale application as an analytic principle may detract from the analysis of key ego and superego activities for those patients who can tolerate such explorations. This can be seen in the following example.

A 25-year-old woman fell silent after I made an interpretation. After a few minutes she said she felt my voice was too "insistent," and she became silent again. I immediately recognized what she was responding to. The interpretation was one that I had speculated about for some time, and the patient's associations confirmed it in a way that she seemed ready to understand. There was, indeed, a shift from my more questioning voice. Returning to this voice, I told the patient that I could see how she heard my voice as different, but wondered about her thoughts of it as "insistent," and why this would cause her to fall silent. The patient's thoughts led her to contrast this more "firm" way of talking with what she contrasted as my "softer" style. She stopped again, realized that she was beginning to feel anxious, and her thoughts then led to various situations that were potentially exciting which she had avoided recently. I could then wonder if it was the "firmness" of my interpretation which she found exciting, but there was something frightening about this which led her to fall silent. This then became another route into understanding the patient's inhibited ego capacities, which led her into analysis because of her job, and the men she became involved with, both of which she found unexciting.

With such a patient, it is tempting to simply turn down the volume of one's voice, thinking that it is her feeling of safety that needs to be guaranteed. However, we must heed Gray's (1991) argument:

> "[U]nless the point is made that methodologies dealing with wider-scope patients represent alternatives required only by analysands who are unanalyzable by more conventional conflict- and resistance-oriented analytic technique, their use may be to discourage or preclude a much wider potential for the analysis of the ego's superego functionings." [p. 14]

AN OBJECT RELATIONS VIGNETTE

Joseph (1988) tells of a patient who began his session by criticizing an older male therapist whom he heard give a lecture. While Joseph comments on the oedipal possibilities in this, she was more struck by the fact that she felt herself being goaded by the patient into an argument whereby Joseph would come to the defense of the other therapist. After Joseph made this interpretation, the patient fell silent. He then described a particularly good piece of work he had done recently. Joseph's explanation for this is that the patient was engaging in "introjective identification" (p. 632).

> Instead of my patient becoming aware that I had opened up something useful and feeling anything about it, he intro-jected this useful object/analyst and, using projective iden-tification, forced the listening, valuing part of his own self into me, then split up and projected into the people lis-tening to his work and praising him. [pp. 632–633]

Striking in the example is how the patient's ego is bypassed completely. What he is aware of, or capable of becoming aware of, seems not to be considered. The interpretation is of what Searl (1936) calls "absent content" (p. 484), which, if used as a primary method of intervention, leaves the patient dependent on the therapist for under-standing what he or she is thinking. "The dynamics of the patient's disability to find his own way have been un-touched" (Searl 1936, p. 479). Even if Joseph's sense of the patient's intent was correct, it is far from his awareness and thus remains as a resistance in action like those originally described by Freud (1914): "For instance, the patient does not say that he remembers that he used to be defiant and critical towards his parents' authority; instead, he behaves in that way to the doctor" (p. 150). To not recognize the resistance elements in the patient's behavior is likely, at best, to increase the resistance. I would see the patient's response to Joseph's remarks as doing to the therapist what he felt was done to him (i.e., saying something about what gave *him* pleasure, but in a way that was unrelated to the therapist's remarks).

CONCLUDING THOUGHTS

Object relations theorists have enriched our understanding of a variety of ego states that play a role in the resistances. With the introduction of such terms as *the false self, the grandiose self, idealized other,* and *splitting,* we have come closer to understanding the specific dangers certain patients feel when faced with accepting, speaking, or even knowing about certain thoughts. These observations provide still another view into the complex adaptations that comprise resistances.

The translation of these insights into an increased understanding of the resistances from an object relations point of view has been less forthcoming. Many give the impression of eschewing resistance interpretations entirely. However, just as the object relations theorists imply that safety is a crucial component for psychotherapists of all persuasions, I would surmise that many object relations theorists are doing resistance analysis while labeling it as something else. Thus, while Winnicott believes "[r]esistance signals the analyst's failure, sometimes in some very simple way, to meet the need arising naturally and legitimately in the evolving analytic setting and relationship" (Fromm 1989, p. 16), from some examples of his clinical work, it is clear he recognized the dangers of working without consideration of the resistances (see especially Winnicott 1968).

Analytic work is a complex and demanding enterprise. As working therapists, faced with a multiplicity of ideas and affects—which are communicated verbally and nonverbally, are both conscious and unconscious for both participants, and allow for a variety of responses—we are constantly tempted with simpler models that reduce ambiguity. By leveling the classical analytic method of resistance analysis to overcoming resistances in order to search out the hidden libido, while simultaneously holding that the patient's sense of safety is due only to breakdowns in analytic empathy, is to search for the unattainable—a less complicated model of human behavior.

I would agree with Weinshel (1992) when he suggests "that the patient's resistance to the analytic work, the analyst's interpretation of that resistance, and the patient's response to that interpretation represented the basic 'unit' of the psychoanalytic process and the core of the analytic work" (p. 334). How closely one holds this view depends on other conceptions one has of the goals of analysis. These include such things as the importance of self-analysis as the goal of psychoanalysis, therapeutic gains and analytic gains, and symptom relief versus the work of analysis as the focus of analysis.

While exploring of each of these issues would take us far afield, a brief foray into one might prove useful. Follow-up studies of completed psychoanalyses (Schlessinger and Robbins 1983) make it clear that conflicts are not obliterated, resolved, or any of the other terms previously used that suggest that analysis did away with conflict. What has become clearer is that even after analysis, conflicts remain alive and ready elements in an individual's psyche. What changes is an individual's ability to respond to the arousal of conflicts in a more adaptive manner. Some process of ongoing self-analysis occurs that allows the individual's ego to respond in new situations of conflict arousal in a more flexible fashion. The limits on the patient's ability for self-analysis are determined by the extent of resistance analysis, especially those resistances to self-analysis. Without resistance analysis we may have a therapeutic analysis, but not a psychoanalysis. As Freud (1910b) notes when discussing the importance of understanding resistances for future psychotherapists:

> [W]e have noticed that no psycho-analyst goes further than his own complexes and *internal resistances* permit; and we consequently require that he shall begin his activity with a self-analysis and continually carry it deeper while he is making his observations on his patients. Anyone who fails to produce results in a self-analysis of this kind may at once give up any idea of being able to treat patients by analysis. [p. 145, italics added]

While expressing himself in a language of a different time and using a quite different meaning of self-analysis, Freud was making the link between the capacity for resistance analysis and self-analysis. As with many of Freud's clinical judgments, his intuitive understanding surpassed his conceptual framework at the time (e.g., his 1895 clinical description of a resistance).

Many types of interventions besides interpretations of resistances are a necessary part of any psychoanalysis. Some of these interventions fit within the category of allowing the patient to feel safe and empathized with, concepts emphasized by many object relations theorists that are important in themselves but also in their contribution to the "other" work of analysis. Increased understanding of the variety of ways patients cope with the traumas in their lives, and the adaptations that derive from these, have also been contributed to greatly by the object relationship theorists. Most therapists accept and see as useful in their daily clinical work the defensive importance of the "false self," "the grandiose self," and the various permutations of real and fantasied object relations that a patient may defensively attempt to create in the analytic session. However, I would maintain that these may be necessary but not sufficient components of a psychoanalysis. They are necessary for the work of analysis to go on but not sufficient in themselves to define a psychoanalysis as either taking or not taking place.

The role the therapist sees for resistance analysis is heavily influenced by what he or she sees as the curative factors in psychoanalysis. Those seeing shifts in the ego as primary tend to focus more on the resistances. Thus, for those like Gray, Loewald (1971, 1975), and me, there is a fundamental shift in thinking as material that was previously unconscious is (after resistance analysis) brought to the attention of the conscious ego. Clinically, this can be seen most clearly in the nature of a patient's thinking in the transference neurosis. For example, the beginning patient who is convinced that the therapist's look shows signs of displeasure can, after a period of analysis, allow his thoughts to be the object of his thinking. In a Piagetian sense, we see in this circumstance a change in thinking from preoperational to representational thinking. The difference is captured by Flavell (1963):

> Piaget likens it [*pre-operational thought*] to a slow-motion film which represents one static frame after another but can give no simultaneous and all-encompassing purview of all the frames. *Representational thought*, on the other hand, through its symbolic capacity has the potential for simultaneously grasping in a single, internal epitome, a whole sweep of separate events. It is a much faster and more mobile device which can recall the past, represent the present, and anticipate the future in one temporally brief, organized act. [p. 152, italics added]

By focusing on resistance analysis, we are looking for those barriers to thoughts being allowed into consciousness. With admission to consciousness, ideas can be approached with levels of thinking heretofore not available to the patient in areas of conflict. This is because in those areas, thought processes remain at some bedrock level (and unconsciously) at a similar developmental stage as when the conflict was first formed. Adult patients in conflict, as Sandler (1975) has pointed out, continue to operate according to childhood laws of cognition and perception. Any new information is fit within this old way of thinking. It is not until modes of thinking in particular areas become conscious, and the reasons for their remaining unconscious are gradually worked on, that new information can be processed at higher levels of ego functioning. Not until we understand the threats that keep particular thoughts and ways of thinking in place can we have a patient move from the slow, static, concrete thinking typical of earlier levels of thought to thought that, among other qualities, is capable of reflecting back on itself. This is the essence of resistance analysis, a basic quality needed for self-analysis, and why I consider analysis of the unconscious ego resistances a *necessary* condition for the establishment of a psychoanalytic process.

10

SCIENCE, LOGIC, AND DISCUSSIONS OF UNCONSCIOUS EGO RESISTANCES

In discussions of the role of the ego in clinical psychoanalysis, and specifically the significance of the unconscious ego in resistances, questions are inevitably raised regarding the role of unconscious gratifications in resistances. The question is usually put in the form of "But you haven't said enough about the role of unconscious wishes or gratification. Do you discount these in the formation of resistances?" This question is asked in spite of stated comments that, for specific reasons, the defense aspect of resistances is being focused on. For example:

> [I]t should be noted at the outset that I see resistances as complex acts with contributions from many sources. The most salient resistances are often found to serve purposes of defense, *drive gratification*, adaptation, and transference. However, it has been the defense aspects of the

Note: This chapter was written with Howard Kamler, Ph.D.

resistances that [have] been most baffling for analysts to
consistently integrate into clinical technique. [Busch 1992,
pp. 1091–1092, italics added]

In this chapter we will suggest that the question is the result
of a failure to appreciate some points of logic and procedure in
science, which may reflect errors in technique, and an eschewing of the role of the ego in clinical psychoanalysis.

Let us begin with a comment on scientific procedure.
Frequently explicit but often implicit in the question on the
role of unconscious gratifications in resistances is the stand
that, in an exposition on resistances, one has left something
out by primarily focusing on the unconscious ego components. It is supposed that in order to do good science, one
ought not to talk about unconscious ego components in
isolation from talk of unconscious gratifications. One should
not investigate connections between ego activity and resistance in isolation from what can be said about unconscious
gratifications' bearing on these same resistances. In other
words, in this view, all aspects of resistances need to be
explicitly related to one another for a genuinely scientific
presentation of the topic.

In fact, discussions of a causal phenomenon (such as the
unconscious ego resistances) in isolation from certain other
causal phenomena (e.g., unconscious gratifications) is the
norm rather than the exception in science. Focusing on an
individual causal phenomenon (and *eventually* seeing how it
is connected to other phenomena) is typically how science
runs. Whole grants, projects, laboratories, and so forth, are
devoted to isolating a given causal phenomenon from other
related causal phenomena, with the goal of seeing all there is
to see about the isolated phenomenon. Indeed, a basic condition of science is to try to rule out the causal interplay of the
phenomenon one is interested in understanding with some of
the other typically related phenomena, in which the very goal
of such an exercise is to see how the phenomenon of interest
behaves in isolation from other phenomena it typically inter-
acts with (Feibleman 1972, Nagel, 1961). It has seemed

crucial to do this with the unconscious ego resistances especially, because of what has clearly been a "developmental lag" (Gray 1982) in integrating the ego into our understanding of working with resistances. And this is no offense to proper scientific procedure.

In fact, the implicit demand to consider the unconscious gratifications in *all* discourse on resistances reflects not only the aforementioned scientific procedural mistake but also certain errors in logic that may reflect errors in technique that have plagued resistance analysis (Busch 1992). When the question is asked, "Why haven't you included the unconscious gratifications in your discussion of resistances?" an assumption is being made that there is a connection between the resistances and unconscious gratification. The question is, "What type of connection is being assumed?" The impression given is that the questioner is *not* arguing a *causal* connection (Carlson-Jones 1983). No one would argue that unconscious ego factors never play a role in psychoanalytic behavior associated with resistances and, conversely, that all resistance behavior can be explained on the basis of unconscious gratifications (although frequently it has been written about in this way). Instead, the questioner seems to be making a *logical* claim—that seeking unconscious gratifications is part of the very meaning of what it is to be a resistance. It is also assumed that investigating this logical aspect of resistance is of paramount importance and that exploring the nuances of defensive unconscious activity is insufficient. The fact is there is a fundamental logical error in play here, and we would like to bring it to the fore now.

At a *theoretical* level, most therapists acknowledge that resistance entails a complex of things—defense components, gratification components, adaptational components, and transference components. What that means is that the *concept* of resistance entails *all* of these components as *necessary logical conditions* (Copi 1990). They are necessary parts of what the concept of resistance *means*. So, just as one might rightly claim that one cannot understand anything about the concept of being a "bachelor" without including an understanding of the idea of being "unmarried" and the idea of being a "male person" (i.e., just as one has to acknowledge that being unmarried and being a man are necessary logical conditions of being a bachelor), so we have to acknowledge the defense component, the gratification component, and so forth, as necessary logical conditions of being a resistance. On a *theoretical* level, all resistances *must* be about defense, gratification, adaptation, and transference.

If we focus on just the gratification and unconscious ego defense necessary conditions (recognizing that what we say here applies to the other components, too), we can sharpen the discussion even more. What is assumed in talk of resistance is that there are (at least) two necessary logical conditions defining it. First, a piece of psychoanalytic behavior is a resistance *only if* that behavior includes, as part of its aim, unconsciously gratifying the patient (e.g., by frustrating the therapist, by making the patient feel omnipotent, by fulfilling sexual urges, etc.). In clinical practice, one would expect to find an unconscious gratification as part of every resistance. For example, all therapists understand that the patient, fearful of telling a dream because of some frightening imagery, may also be negating the therapist's capacity to understand dreams and unconsciously attempting to destroy the therapist. Thus, while the height of clinical acumen is expressed in the therapist's sensitivity to which aspect of a resistance needs elaboration at any one moment, at a *theoretical* level there is a *logical* connection between resistances and unconscious gratifications.

Again, though, this is not the *only* necessary logical condition of resistance. Importantly, the second condition is that a piece of psychoanalytic behavior is a resistance *only if* that behavior is *also* aimed at defending the ego from some perceived threat—that is, *only if* it also expresses the ego's unconscious concern with avoiding knowing about something that threatens its existence.

A tendency to see the first condition as the *primary* logical condition in resistance formation is related to the long time that Freud's thinking was dominated by his first theory of anxiety (i.e., anxiety as the result of dammed-up libido) and his (and many subsequent psychotherapists') difficulty in adapting his second theory of anxiety into usable clinical technique. Quite importantly, each view has had its clinical ramifications for the treatment of resistance. In the context of the first condition, the common clinical practice has been to treat the resistance as something to bypass. The therapist is convinced to go right for uncovering the unconscious gratification fantasies so as to get past the stubborn resistance. The patient is thereby given the subtle message that resistances are unacceptable roadblocks.

It has primarily been through the work of Gray that this approach has begun to be ameliorated. Yet, when the question of why unconscious gratifications have not been included in discussions of the resistance is asked, it reflects an error that has plagued psychoanalysis for some time—that is, treating the first condition as though it were the *primary necessary* condition of resistance, not one among many equally significant conditions for a resistance to occur.

Another reason that questions regarding the unconscious gratifications come up in discussions of the unconscious ego's role in resistances is that, in fact, the psychoanalytic community has created another connection, besides a logical one, between resistance and unconscious gratification. It has created a *conventional* connection (Kuhn 1970) between them. That is, it is a sociological fact that therapists have adopted the convention of demanding that talk about resistances include discussion of gratification seeking. While it has been pointed out that this stance is due to an overemphasis on libidinal gratifications in the resistances, with a corresponding neglect of the unconscious ego, a sociological norm has been established that says one must *emphasize* unconscious gratifications in discussing the resistances. That is, discussions of resistances have been historically tilted toward highlighting the role of unconscious gratifications in the establishment and resolution of resistances.

Thus, the fate of the resistances have been *conventionally* connected with unconscious gratification, and not to underline these in a discussion of resistances is to break with convention.

Characteristic of the conventional connection is this recent definition of resistances:

> Once the patient's unconscious conflicts have been uncovered and some insights obtained, resistances may lead to delay or even failure to progress, reflecting an unconsciously determined reluctance to give up inappropriate childhood wishes and their maladaptive, defensively distorted expressions in symptoms, character, or behavior. [Moore and Fine 1990, p. 169]

In this definition, resistance is intimately linked with unconscious gratification, not only logically, but also through the *convention-determined* assumption that lack of progress in analysis is based on continued gratification seeking rather than failing to explore sufficiently the feelings of danger associated with the ego unconsciously instituting stringent measures of resistance to change.

Now, following Freud, that psychotherapists should have formed a convention favoring a focus on unconscious gratifications, and not on unconscious ego threats, is just of historical and sociological interest. It has no logical currency. One condition simply is not inherently more important than the other in understanding and working with resistances. Freud's (1923, 1926) late discovery of the ego's role in resistances, and his difficulty in fully integrating it into his clinical thinking, have been other contributions to our only episodic grasping of the importance of the threat to the unconscious ego in the formation of resistances. Freud placed more clinical emphasis on his first theory of anxiety, which led to the subsequent connection between resistances and the unconscious gratifications behind them. This fact has led to an overemphasis on the role of unconscious gratifications and a lack of appreciation for the role of the unconscious ego in resistances.

But logic does not bow to historic accident. Concepts have the logical condition they have regardless of the historic conventions that may have grown up around them. We should therefore not be dictated to by convention when we are trying to clarify concepts. We should focus instead on the necessary conditions—indeed, on all the necessary conditions. Accordingly, it is important to highlight that gratification and unconscious ego activity have the same logical status in understanding the resistances; that is, they are both necessary conditions.

At a *clinical* level, it is *imperative* to distinguish between the role of the unconscious ego and unconscious gratifications. If the patient is expressing signs of threat and the therapist interprets the unconscious gratification behind the threat, we have missed the opportunity for an experience-near analysis of the unconscious ego. Differences in approach can be seen in how the therapist deals with the patient's telling, with many pauses, a masturbatory fantasy. At a theoretical level there is little doubt that there is a logical connection between the pauses (resistances), and whatever unconscious gratifications are in the masturbatory fantasy, and what is being expressed in action via the manner the fantasy is being told. From the side of the ego, too, however, there is also a logical connection with resistance. So there is considerable merit in focusing on the fact that a resistance is evident, as well as keeping in mind the form, meaning, history, and adaptiveness of the resistance. It has been this aspect of the resistances that has remained relatively unexplored. This approach, which brings the ego to center stage of the analysis, is based on Gray's (1990) transformation of Freud's aphorism "where unconscious ego was, conscious ego shall be"(p. 1095). We would concur with Gray's (1982) belief that "the therapeutic results of analytic treatment are lasting in proportion to the extent which, during the analysis, the patient's unbypassed ego functions have become involved in a consciously and increasingly voluntary co-partnership with the analyst" (p. 624).

We would like to conclude our argument by suggesting

an analogy that may highlight the logical points we have been making about what in fact goes on and what ought to go on with resistances, unconscious gratifications, and unconscious ego activities. Suppose, as an automotive engineer for BMW, you learn that the QZ-97 chemical additive in the gasoline supply is a necessary condition for optimal performance. So you study the sources of QZ-97, the best way to get it into gasoline, why it affects good performance, and the ways the absence of the additive interferes with a BMW's optimal performance. Other automotive engineers may become so enamored with the role played by QZ-97 for optimal BMW functioning, that the convention among them might come to be expressed in the necessity to say, "If you're going to talk about the high-speed performance of a BMW, you've just got to say something about QZ-97." However, even so, someone would not be wrong in looking at (and for) other (new) necessary conditions for optimal performance. Certainly there are other conditions that affect performance (i.e., the aerodynamic flow of the design, the types of tires, the number of cylinders, etc.). One is simply saying there are other necessary conditions to BMW performance that need to be looked at if we are really interested in maximizing the chances of getting BMWs to perform at high speeds optimally. If we stuck with the convention of just focusing on the complex behaviors of QZ-97, we would learn a good deal about QZ-97 and its causal effect on optimal performance, but we would make no progress in understanding *all* there is to know about optimal performance.

It seems apparent that convention has led therapists to the position of saying, "When you talk about resistances, you need to say something about unconscious gratifications." However, what we have been arguing in this chapter is that it is important also to look at the workings of all the necessary conditions if we are really interested in maximizing the work of analysis. Moreover, it is important to focus on the unconscious ego in isolation from its relationship with gratification to help point to its relative neglect in the literature and also to mirror the way it needs, at times, to be at the center of analytic work for the most effective ego analysis to take place.

11

A SAMPLE FROM A SUPERVISED CASE

As explained by Apfelbaum and Gill (1989), it is sometimes easier to demonstrate certain problems or characteristics of technique using clinical material other than one's own. To show the tendencies to bypass resistances, interpret out of the "neighborhood," not use the material of free association in a closely monitored fashion, and to interpret actions without consideration of the form of the communication, as well as many other technical inclinations noted throughout this book, an advanced candidate has been gracious enough to allow me to use material from our supervisory work. It isn't that I don't continue to struggle with these same issues in my own work. However, supervision gives me the opportunity to chronicle the frequency of such tendencies more systematically at this point.

The candidate whose material we will be looking at is a gifted one, close to graduation, with an openness to learning and a keen interest in examining issues of technique. The issues that arise are those that I have inevitably encountered in clinical discussions with therapists at every level. I raise this point to counteract what will be a tendency for many to dismiss what I will be discussing as irrelevant to them, since the work is that of a candidate. In frequent presentations around the country, I am often assured therapists do not do this kind of work "here," only to hear clinical material demonstrating the relevance of my presentation to "here." To me, such an attitude illustrates the discrepancy between the intuitive wisdom of an analytic approach highlighting the ego and the pull from other factors noted earlier in these chapters (e.g., the magnetic power of the unconscious fantasies associated with instinctual derivatives, and the therapist's authoritarian stance).

We will pick up the clinical material approximately six months into the analysis. The material may, upon reading, appear fragmented, which reflects the candidate's method of reporting but is more a result of the patient's uneasiness. Many topics represent the mental equivalent of touching a hot stove. Thus, the main thrust of my remarks will revolve around the necessity of resistance interpretations. However, the same close reading of the text and elaboration of observable data are applicable for the elucidation of unconscious fantasies. For the purpose of understanding the material to be presented, all that need be known is that the patient is a man in his mid-forties, with a successful business and a second marriage with no children. He came into treatment because of his feelings of social isolation and a previous history of building up successful businesses only to have them fail.

SESSION 1

The patient was five minutes late, describing it as due to his needing to stay at work for a discussion with some of his employees. He mentioned that it is tough to look at this relationship (with the therapist) and wonders, "What's in it for you?" He then recalled a former consultant to his business that started to work with computers. He stopped using him, because he got greedy and developed questionable ethics. He likes the therapist and feels like he bonded with him. It makes him emotional to think the therapist gets something emotional from him. He wonders whether it is like what he feels about his employees. He hopes the therapist will really like him. *I said, however, that these wishes must be conflictual and difficult for him and may have accounted for his being late.* He laughed, and said that he knew the therapist would not miss that. He was uncomfortable to think there was something about him that made him unlikable. It makes him hold back. He then recalled how inconsistent his mother was. He described the therapist as very consistent, but he still had fears about letting his hair down too much, trusting too much. It is really nice the therapist is so consistent. *But you're afraid I might become inconsistent.* He recalled talking some time ago about his concern the therapist might leave the area.

He has thought recently how it would be nice to have kids. It's nice to be surrounded by his employees. He generally keeps people at arm's length. He then described a number of acquaintances who had invited him to do something, but he always refused. He was afraid they would think something is the matter with him and wouldn't like him. He's like his mother, but he added he doesn't like the way his mother always needs to be the center of attention. She can be nice but isn't. As a child, he was a bossy little shit. He didn't know there was another way to be. He has tried to be different as an adult. He tries to be fair and reasonable, although he can be mean and difficult. When it comes to selling, he has balls of steel. He sold life insurance in college and was good at it. However, he added, it was probably the beer that did it. He's worried that his social inhibition will be difficult to overcome. He then mentioned he would have difficulty making an appointment the next week. *The therapist then wondered whether he was concerned that he (the therapist) would affect him the way his mother did, which accounted for his lateness today.* He agreed. He wondered whether it would help him to read about this stuff. It seemed a little confusing. He would like to do it better, and faster.

DISCUSSION OF SESSION 1

After arriving five minutes late for his appointment, the patient wonders what the therapist is getting out of the treatment. His thoughts then turn to firing his business consultant, because he became greedy and had questionable ethics. He immediately switches to how much he likes the therapist. The patient ends up talking about how much he hopes the therapist likes him. The therapist's first intervention is to contradict the patient. In essence, he states that the patient may think he wants the therapist to like him (the patient), but it is much more "difficult" and "conflictual" than the patient has any idea of. The only evidence offered for this view is the patient's arriving five minutes late, a piece of data the patient has already explained in another fashion. Thus, this first intervention is an example of the therapist acting as an authority—that is, telling the patient he may think he is thinking one way, but the therapist can see he is acting in an entirely different manner. Furthermore, the patient's understanding of a piece of behavior (coming late) is disregarded, with no explanation, and superseded by the therapist's reading of this same piece of behavior.

I have no difference with the candidate as to what the issues are that the patient is bringing into this session, which is generally the case in supervision. The therapist is in the ballpark as to the underlying conflicts, but there are major differences in how best to bring this to the patient's attention in a way that he will find most usable. I would begin by recounting with the patient how he started to wonder what I, the therapist, was getting out of the session, then talked of his greedy consultant, and immediately switched to how much he liked me. I would suggest there was some uneasiness in his linking the consultant with me, which led to his need to undo this connection. If the patient was able to grasp what I was saying to this point, I would wonder with him whether he was aware of any thought or feeling immediately preceding the undoing as a beginning investigation of the specific dangerous affect driving the resistance. In this manner, I would use the data most easily available to the patient, *his own words*, to highlight the resistance to his connection between the consultant and me. It is truly a Grayian moment.

This is a conflict in action, not some hypothesized conflict based on the patient coming late. It is data available to both the patient and therapist. The discovery of meaning in the patient's associations is frequently found via listening carefully to the patient's associations. The purpose of the intervention, in this case, would be the investigation of those factors that have led to the resistance. What is disconcerting to the patient about the connection between the consultant and the therapist that leads him to need to skitter away from it? The therapist's actual intervention does not invite an investigation of the resistance. Rather, its purpose is to explain a piece of behavior (i.e., coming late), which the patient does not have a question about. In short, the intervention demonstrates a number of the interpretive ills described in these chapters. While the therapist is not in the patient's "neighborhood," we also see the him handling the resistance in the mode of the "developmental lag" and directly interpreting the resistance elements of an action as a classic way of breaking through the resistances.

The therapist's second intervention is of a type I hear frequently. It seems to be a misinterpretation of Gill's (1982) views on interpreting the transference, in which anything the patient says about another person is taken as a statement about the therapist. Furthermore, presenting a transference interpretation to the patient without further support as to how the therapist came to such a view leads, at best, to a highly intellectualized understanding of the transference. The patient begins to think of his associations as the therapist does— as a simple code in which anytime someone's name is mentioned, it is automatically translated to mean "transference," without any of the usual displacement of subject and object.

Finally, the intervention suffers from many of the same ills described in the first intervention. If I were to comment here, it would be to note how the patient switched from talking about the therapist and his possible connection to the consultant with questionable ethics, to his own (the patient's) unlikableness. In essence, the resistance to his thoughts about the therapist are still in evidence, with his concerns about the therapist now internalized. Pointing out the patient's transferences in the face of a resistance to just this idea will, of course, not be particularly helpful to the patient. In addition, such an approach frequently ends up in a type of intellectualized defensive reaching to the past that ends up with little that is illuminating to the patient or therapist.

In the therapist's final intervention, he again tries to make a connection between what the patient is talking about and the therapist, in the ways described earlier. What is still being ignored is the patient's resistance to this connection. The patient's internalization of complaints about the therapist, and his defensive use of the past have continued throughout the session. The patient's confusion about the therapist's methods are evident in his comments at the end of the session, when he wonders whether he should read something about "this stuff" to help clarify what is going on.

SESSION 2

The patient had a great weekend. He played golf and went canoeing. He placed second in the golf tournament. Although canoeing was pretty good, he and his wife had some problems. Whenever they got into a difficult place, she would paddle first and think second. He talked with a couple of his business suppliers over the weekend. They got a contract worked out. It was really neat. He also had an office worker quit over the weekend. That hurt. There were a few other problems at work, but he had a really good weekend. He is glad his wife is working in his office, so now they can talk more about business. His golf game started out really badly. He hopes his partner wants to play with him again. He put on tape what was talked about in analysis last week. He needs to be on time and committed. *I asked him whether he felt I had said this or otherwise indicated he wasn't doing this treatment correctly.* The patient answered in the negative but added that he still ended up feeling this way.

What really bugged him was the problem canoeing with his wife and losing at golf. She would paddle without thinking, and he started yelling at her. Also, he hates to lose at golf. He was pleased he didn't have any temper tantrums even with his rocky play. He hasn't made love to his wife in a long time. They talked about it some and may have to try some new things. He was really glad he got that big truck for her. He feels much better about her safety. *I asked whether he noticed that talking about his observations about last time made him anxious.* He did recall talking about his relationship with the therapist. He seems to have trouble with that. Anytime he talks about the two-sided nature of this relationship, he becomes anxious. It's like with his golf partner. He really cares what this guy thinks of him. At the golf tournament he realized he doesn't make small talk well. He used to be good at it. So the therapist is like his golf partner in some way. He worries sometimes, when they play as a team, that he may let this guy down. *I think you may also feel you let me down.* Yeah, like being late the other day and missing a number of appointments over the next few weeks. *But you are suggesting, like with your golf partner, I will be disappointed, critical, and not want to work with you.* He feels afraid to talk about it. It's best to leave well enough alone. He never got consistent feedback from his mother. He really wants to move forward here. He needs to be more trusting. He must experience the therapist like his mother—critical. He really didn't want to come in second in the golf tournament.

DISCUSSION OF SESSION 2

In the therapist's first comment, he once again speaks to the transference, without explanation as to how he had come to this question/interpretation. Even if the therapist is correct, he has given the patient little help in understanding the basic mechanisms of the analytic process whereby there is some organicity between what the patient and therapist are doing. It is as if the therapist's interventions were divined, and it is only via his special powers that such understanding can be obtained. Yet, as I have pointed out throughout these chapters, if a goal of psychoanalysis is self-analysis, then we must be able to demonstrate to the patient how analysis works. While I might also have a question as to how the patient had come to his conclusion about the need for greater commitment, I would ask, "How had he come to this conclusion?" In this way, we evidence our interest in the patient's thinking, which is one essential element of what psychoanalysis has to offer (i.e., the patient's ability to be interested in his thoughts as a reflection of decreased resistance and as a method of understanding conflict).

My own intervention would center around noting that every time the patient mentioned a problem, this was quickly followed by some upbeat news. The problem with canoeing is followed by the contract's working out. The description of the difficulties at work are ended with a repetition of what a great weekend it was. Once again I would be attempting to show the patient there is a resistance in operation, this time to the more generic issue of "problems." To interpret some problem (e.g., the patient experiencing the therapist as critical of him) at this point, is to fly in the face of just what the patient is most resistant to at this moment.

The patient then tries to define what did bother him over the weekend and specifies the difficulties with his wife and his golf game. His anger is salient in both situations, and this is followed by another reaction formation in which what is highlighted in his description of the truck he bought for his wife are its protective capabilities. His dwindling sexual encounters with his wife are related by him to his struggles with his anger toward her. Thus, in the midst of the resistance, there is a brief deepening of the material as the patient elaborates the affect to which the resistances are attached.

Once again we have an example of a resistance in action that needs to be brought to the patient's attention for the analysis to move forward. Furthermore, one can see how crucial this would be in his understanding of painful life experiences he is becoming aware of. Where the investigation needs to start, and what he is demonstrating, is his difficulty in allowing himself to keep in mind his angry thoughts and feelings. This is what gets short-circuited, as the patient experiences some danger from these feelings. Thus, I would say to the patient that what he describes as his two biggest problems involved situations in which he was concerned about his anger. He connects this with the diminution of his sexual activity with his wife, and then ends up talking about how glad he is that he bought his wife this safe vehicle, which suggests an uneasiness in keeping in mind his angry thoughts. I would then wonder with him whether he was aware of any discomfort at the point he began to talk of his wife's safety. Instead, the therapist makes a connection between the mention of the previous session and the patient's anxiety. It is obscure how the therapist came to this conclusion. The patient then returns to putting himself down and praising the therapist. As seen in the previous session, this occurred when he was having negative thoughts about the therapist, and we can assume a similar process is going on. My thoughts on the therapist's direct translation of the transference are similar to those mentioned in the discussion of the first section.

SESSION 3

The patient came into town with his wife today. The suspension on her truck may be too stiff. She almost lost control of it last night. He may need to take it back to the dealer and get a new one. She is having surgery for fat removal next month. His business is slightly in the red at this point. He woke up this morning thinking about it. It bugs him, even though he knows it's temporary. One of his office staff is leaving, which worries him. Things are a little tight in the office. He recalled talking recently about his not being late and making his appointment. His wife talked about her group therapy today. She's doing pretty well with it. He's worried about going on vacation, when he is a little short staffed at work. However, things are really good in the warehouse. He's concerned about all the changes his consultant wishes to make. On the other hand, there is no way he will make less than $250,000 this year. It's exciting.

I asked him whether he was aware of feeling anxious. He said he was. He couldn't recall what we had talked about in treatment yesterday. He thought it was about his being late and gone a lot. He also talked about the relationship, that he guessed the therapist could be doing this for more than just money. He was going to put on a tape but got to talking with his wife. A friend of hers said she thought the patient's wife had a great marriage. It made him anxious to think how tight money was this month at his business. He wonders whether he should be looking at the condo that he's thinking of buying. Should he be worried about the money? Maybe it's all the changes here. He's on uncomfortable ground. *What is he thinking this is about?* Well, it's more than just a business. He worries about acceptance. He has trouble fitting into his country club, but others have similar concerns. He goes on to talk about golf and in actuality how he probably has enough money to retire right now if he wanted to.

I pointed out how he had difficulty looking into his feelings here and wondered what thoughts he had about it. He said he wasn't sure where to go with it. He feels it's easier to skirt the issue. It's like asking a girl out on a date. He fears rejection. He recalled looking for a golf partner. He asked three guys before he found somebody. It makes him feel vulnerable. It's more comfortable to lie here and speak about other things. He recalled talking in the past about being lonely as a kid. He wondered whether the therapist thought less of him. He can be very self-critical. He feels unacceptable. *I told him I thought he imagined I would have these same critical, unaccepting feelings toward him.* He really doesn't like it when he thinks others are critical of him. He has really enjoyed the friendships he and his wife have been developing with other couples recently. They have had some good times.

It feels like he is putting a lot on the line here. He could lose somehow, feel unacceptable. If he calls people to play golf, and they can't, it really hurts his feelings. *I pointed out that some part of these feelings must be related to our having to change our appointment for tomorrow. But experiencing this as part of the acceptable–unacceptable conflict makes him feel he is putting a lot on the line. Hence, he needed to keep it outside of awareness.* He recalled how in college he had two dates with women he really wanted to go out with. He was really excited, but both canceled.

DISCUSSION OF SESSION 3

The therapist's first intervention is based on the observation of the patient's increased anxiety. The therapist asks an important question: is the patient aware of his anxiety? It is important in that one cannot proceed in an investigation of the anxiety until there is an agreement with the patient that this, indeed, is what he is feeling. This first step (agreement between the patient and therapist on what the feeling is) is too frequently ignored in the interpretation of feelings. Unfortunately, once again, the therapist fails to explain where his awareness of the patient's anxiety comes from. The patient hasn't said anything about feeling anxious. We have no evidence of discomfort expressed motorically. The patient has been left in the dark as to how the therapist has come to his conclusions. Thus, his inclusion in the process as a coparticipant in the investigation of his thoughts and feelings has, at best, not been aided. The model of the therapist as mind reader is being perpetuated. The data the therapist is responding to is the intensification of the patient's style of flitting from topic to topic. Thus, the anxiety can be seen in the manner in which the patient is using the method of free association.

This is tricky to interpret, especially in the early part of treatment, without having the patient feeling criticized or making the patient more self-conscious of the process and contributing to greater inhibition. I will frequently make mention of this method of working in my opening remarks to a patient (e.g., "Sometimes we will be interested not only in your thoughts, but how your thoughts come out.") and refer back to it when I make my first intervention about the process (e.g., "When I first talked with you about how it might be best to proceed, I mentioned that sometimes we would be looking at your method of telling us what's on your mind."). With this as a background, I might say to the patient something like, "I notice that today you seemed to be moving more quickly from topic to topic, as if you were uneasy about something. I wonder if you are aware of feeling uneasy." If the patient agrees, I would then wait to see where his or her associations led. It is a technique that can only be used sparingly, especially in the beginning phase of analysis. The patient's narcissistic vulnerability at these times leads him or her to experience this focus, if it occurs too frequently, as a criticism, which can result in an interference in the freedom of associations. This is why with those patients who, from early in the analysis, have the propensity to express their conflicts more in the action of talking rather than via the content, it is sometimes necessary to be more authoritarian while actually being more therapeutic.

The patient gives some indication of what his anxiety might be about when, later in the session after the therapist suggests that he was finding it difficult to look into his feelings, the patient associated to how it "feels easier to skirt the issues" and he feels like "asking a girl on a date." He likens it to inviting someone to be his golf partner, and then connects this back to the relationship with the therapist. He seems to be suggesting his anxiety has to do with seeing his male analyst in terms of male–female relationships. This issue arises again when, after the therapist focuses on the patient's discomfort with feelings about the changed appointment time, the patient again goes to a time when two women he was excited to go out with canceled dates with him.

While there are many unknowns about this (i.e., what are the specifics of his concern, how conscious of them is he), the issue is most easily approached from the specifics of the patient's associations. It is one of those times it is difficult to know whether one is dealing with an unconscious resistance or what Kris (1982) calls a "reluctance." The latter is when the patient is conscious of a certain hesitation to delve into a topic. By staying closely tied to the patient's associations, we are staying within the process to explain our conclusions. We say, "From your words you seem to be saying such and such about your uneasiness." In this manner we are not imposing a meaning primarily from somewhere other than what the patient can be easily conscious of (i.e., the patient's own words). If we are dealing with a resistance rather than a reluctance, the patient will correct us. I would return the patient to the question that stimulated the thoughts (i.e., What was making it difficult to look into his feelings?) and remind him that what came to mind had to do with male–female relationships. While he was thinking of this example in terms of rejection (and indeed this concern had been discussed many times before), he was adding this specific dimension that might further help explain his anxiety.

The therapist's final transference interpretation of this hour (i.e., the patient's hurt feelings are also related to the therapist's inability to meet at their regular time the following day) has a number of problems, which have already been addressed. If the connections were more firmly made (i.e., "You mention feeling put on the line here, and then describe feeling hurt when golfing partners have other plans. Since I've had to change our plans for tomorrow, I wonder if you're alluding to that, but that some feelings associated with these thoughts make you uneasy.") and the defense process were highlighted, it would come closer to what I might attempt to say in this situation. The candidate is in the right ballpark, but the lack of connection to the patient's thoughts in the interpretation, as well as the resistance not being highlighted but rather added on as an observation (i.e., "has needed to keep it out of awareness"), with no attempt to explore its causes, is what differentiates the candidate's manner of interpreting from mine. It is the feelings of being hurt in the context of the patient's male–female feelings toward the therapist that make this dangerous, not the feelings of hurt per se. The patient is acknowledging feeling hurt and vulnerable with the therapist. The question is why the specifics of the time change did not come to his mind. This is the point of departure for the investigation of the resistance.

SESSION 4

The patient played golf with some of his suppliers. He had a lot of fun. He was listening to a tape on the way in today, and he was reminded of his concerns that the therapist would reject him. He has this perception that analysis is going slowly. He likes it better when it's going fast. *Going slowly?* He seems to be struggling with the same thing. He spoke with his mother on the phone, and she invited them for dinner. He liked that. So, something has changed there. He's not sure what. His cash flow looks better today. He'is feeling more comfortable with the money. He was turned down for a big loan by one of the banks, and this really pissed him off. He'll get the money from another bank. They decided to keep his wife's truck—just put new shocks and struts in it. He's feeling better about finishing second in the golf tournament. He went on to talk more about golf and the business.

Things are going really well in his life. Lots of changes are occurring, and it's exciting. It bugs him that he and L. (his wife) don't make love. They're both really very busy. He's looking forward to his vacation. L. says they'll make love every day. So, at least she's thinking about it. When he played golf the other night, his wife was another guy's partner. He didn't enjoy playing against her and would rather have had her as his partner. His wife really enjoyed herself. He felt very competitive with this guy whose wife doesn't play golf. He noticed he felt some jealousy. He does not like anyone messing with his wife. His wife said her golf partner wasn't her kind of guy, but he wasn't so sure. He went back to work issues, condo buying, other real estate deals, and so forth. He really enjoys his wife being in the business. There is no conflict there. More about taxes, cash flow, and so on.

This brings him back to his relationship with the therapist. He thinks things are really going well here. He then returned to talking about his business. *I noticed there are two sets of associations, those that include me and those that leave me out.* The patient could see it, although the stuff with L. and golf was difficult to discuss. His friend invited them to go to the football game. He declined. This guy is a better golfer than him. *I said I thought he didn't want to feel certain feelings with me, especially competitive feelings. This, I thought, led him to leave me out of the picture some times in his talking.* He agreed.

DISCUSSION OF SESSION 4

In this session, the therapist attempts to use the process to make an interpretation. He astutely notes that the patient isolates discussions of the relationship from the rest of what he is discussing. While I fully agree with the therapist's observation, I would bring it to the patient's attention just at the moment when he attempted to bring the two sets of thoughts together, but then needed to move away. This occurred toward the end of the session when, after the patient talked about his jealousy again, he states, "Which gets us back to my relationship with you" and then moved away. At this moment we see, once again, the conflict in action, and thus, it is most easily demonstrated to the patient rather than a more abstract formulation. I would say something like, "I had noticed that when you talked you had two types of thoughts, those that related to the relationship with me, and those that were outside thoughts. When you tried to bring the two together, as you just did, your thoughts quickly moved away. It was as if to bring the two sets of thoughts together made you uneasy." I would then go on to ask him what he might have been aware of before his thoughts moved away.

Given the theme of the previous session, there is a question in my mind as to whether the patient is competing *with* or *for* his wife. When the patient described having "competitive" feelings, I might have asked him to elaborate. One is likely to find out just as much, however, by seeing what thoughts come to mind when the resistance noted earlier is pointed out. This has the advantage of staying within the associative model, although an occasional clarifying question does no damage to this model as long as one does not ask a question that is, in reality, an attempt to confirm an already held idea. This latter point is seen frequently. When the therapist does not get the desired answer, he or she makes the interpretation held in the first place.

The therapist ends this session by highlighting the resistance to a certain feeling. While I might disagree with the specifics of what he might be interpreting, he is now much closer to the patient's "neighborhood." He is staying closer to the process and attempting to point out a connection the patient is loath to stay with.

REFERENCES

Abend, S. M. (1990). The influence of the patient's previous knowledge on the opening phase. In *On Beginning an Analysis*, ed. T. Jacobs and A. Rothstein, pp. 57–66. Madison, CT: International Universities.

Anthi, P. R. (1983). Reconstruction of preverbal experience. *Journal of the American Psychoanalytic Association* 31:33–59.

Apfelbaum, B. (1962). Some problems in contemporary ego psychology. *Journal of the American Psychoanalytic Association* 10:526–537.

Apfelbaum, B., and Gill, M. M. (1989). Ego analysis and the relativity of defense: Technical implications of the structural theory. *Journal of the American Psychoanalytic Association* 37:1071–1096.

Arlow, J. A. (1975). The structural hypothesis: technical considerations. *Psychoanalytic Quarterly*. 44:509–525.

_____ (1985). The concept of psychic reality and related problems. *Journal of the American Psychoanalytic Association* 33:521–526.

Arlow, J. A., and Brenner, C. (1990). The psychoanalytic process. *Psychoanalytic Quarterly* 59:678–692.

Balint, M. (1950). Changing therapeutic aims and techniques in psycho-analysis. *International Journal of Psycho-Analysis* 31:117–124.

Blum, H. (1981). The forbidden guest and the analytic ideal: the superego and insight. *Psychoanalytic Quarterly* 50:535–556.

Boesky, D. (1982). Acting out: a reconsideration of the concept. *International Journal of Psycho-Analysis* 63:39–55.

_____ (1990). The psychoanalytic process and its components. *Psychoanalytic Quarterly* 59:550–584.

_____ (1992). *The counter-transference and the resistance: The impossible terms of the impossible profession.* Paper presented at a meeting of the Michigan Psychoanalytic Society, Southfield, MI, February.

Brenner, C. (1982). *The Mind in Conflict.* New York: International Universities Press.

_____ (1990). On beginning an analysis. In *On Beginning an Analysis,* ed. T. Jacobs and A. Rothstein, pp. 47–56. Madison, CT: International Universities Press.

Buie, D. (1993). *The borderline patient: a therapeutic approach to conflicts, deficits, and needs for maturation.* Paper presented at a meeting of the Association for the Advancement of Psychoanalysis, Southfield, MI, October.

Busch, F. (1989). The compulsion to repeat in action: a developmental perspective. *International Journal of Psycho-Analysis* 70:535–544.

_____ (1992). Recurring thoughts on the unconscious ego resistances. *Journal of the American Psychoanalytic Association* 40:1089–1115.

_____ (1993). In the neighborhood: aspects of a good interpretation and its relationship to a "developmental lag" in ego psychology. *Journal of the American Psychoanalytic Association* 41:151–178.

_____ (1994). Some ambiguities in the method of free association and their implications for technique. *Journal of the American Psychoanalytic Association*n 42:363–384.

_____ (1995a). An unknown classic: M. N. Searl's (1936) "Some Queries on Principles of Technique." *Psychoanalytic Quarterly* 64 (in press).

_____ (1995b). Resistance analysis and object relations theory: erroneous conceptions amidst some timely contributions. *Psychoanalytic Psychology* 12:43–53.

_____ (1995c). Do actions speak louder than words? A query into an enigma in analytic theory and technique. *Journal of the American Psychoanalytic Association.* 43 (in press).

_____ (1995d). Beginning a psychoanalytic treatment: establishing an analytic frame. *Journal of the American Psychoanalytic Association* (in press).

Calef, V. (1982). An introspective on training and nontraining analysis. *Annual of Psychoanalysis* 10:93–114.

Carlson-Jones, M. (1983). *Introduction to Logic*. New York: McGraw-Hill.

Chused, J. F. (1991). The evocative power of enactments. *Journal of the American Psychoanalytic Association* 39:615–640.

Copi, I. (1990). *Introduction to Logic*. New York: Macmillan.

Davison, W. T., Bristol, C., and Pray, M. (1986). Turning aggression on the self: a study of psychoanalytic process. *Psychoanalytic Quarterly* 55:273–295.

Davison, W. T., Pray, M., and Bristol, C. (1990). Mutative interpretation and close process minitoring in a study of psychoanalytic process. *Psychoanalytic Quarterly* 59:599–628.

Deutsch, F. (1947). Analysis of postural behavior. *Psychoanalytic Quarterly* 16:195–213.

_____ (1952). Analytic posturology. *Psychoanalytic Quarterly* 21:196–214.

Dewald, P. A. (1980). The handling of resistances in adult psychoanalysis. *International Journal of Psycho-Analysis* 61:61–70.

Downey, T. W. (1987). Notes on play and guilt in child analysis. *Psychoanalytic Study of the Child* 42:105–126. New Haven, CT: Yale University Press.

Eissler, K. R. (1965). *Medical Orthodoxy and the Future of Psychoanalysis* New York: International Universities Press

Emde, R. N. (1988). Development terminable and interminable. II. Recent psychoanalytic theory and therapeutic considerations. *International Journal of Psycho-Analysis* 69:283–296.

—— (1991). Positive emotions for psychoanalytic theory: surprises from infancy research and new directions. *Journal of the American Psychoanalytic Association* Supp:5–44.

Epstein, G. (1976). A note on the semantic confusion in the fundamental rule of psychoanalysis. *Journal of the Philadelphia Association of Psychoanalysis* 3:54–57.

Erikson, E. H. (1963). *Identity and the Life Cycle.* New York: Norton.

Feibleman, J. K. (1972). *Scientific Method.* The Hague: Martin Nijhoff.

Fenichel, O. (1941). *Problems of Psychoanalytic Technique.* New York: Psychoanalytic Quarterly.

Flavell, J. H. (1963). *The Developmental Psychology of Jean Piaget.* Princeton, NJ: Van Nostrand.

Fogel, G. I. (1989). The authentic function of psychoanalytic theory: an overview of the contributions of Hans Loewald. *Psychoanalytic Quarterly* 58:419–451.

Freud, A. (1936). *The Ego and the Mechanisms of Defence.* New York: International Universities Press, 1946.

—— (1946). *The Psycho-Analytical Treatment of Children.* London: Imago.

—— (1965a). *Normality and Pathology in Childhood.* New York: International Universities Press.

—— (1965b). Diagnostic skills and their growth in psychoanalysis. *International Journal of Psycho-Analysis* 46:31–38.

_____ (1968). Acting out. *International Journal of Psycho-Analysis* 49:165–170.

Freud, S. (1895). Studies on Hysteria. *Standard Edition* 2.

_____ (1900). The interpretation of dreams. *Standard Edition* 4 and 5.

_____ (1910). "Wild" psycho-analysis. *Standard Edition* 11:219–230.

_____ (1910b). Future prospects of psychoanalysis. *Standard Edition* 11:139–152.

_____ (1912a). The dynamics of the transference. *Standard Edition* 12:97–108.

_____ (1912b). Recommendations to physicians practising psycho-analysis. *Standard Edition* 12:109–120.

_____ (1913). On beginning the treatment: further recommendations on the technique of psycho-analysis. I. *Standard Edition* 12:121–144.

_____ (1914). Remembering, repeating, and working through. *Standard Edition* 12:145–156.

_____ (1915). The unconscious. *Standard Edition* 14:159–216.

_____ (1917a). Introductory lectures on psycho-analysis. Transference. *Standard Edition* 16:431–447.

_____ (1917b). Introductory lectures on psycho-analysis. Analytic therapy. *Standard Edition* 16:448–463.

_____ (1923). The ego and the id. *Standard Edition* 19:3–68.

_____ (1926). Inhibitions, symptoms, and anxieties. *Standard Edition* 20:77–178.

_____ (1932). New introductory lectures. *Standard Edition* 22.

_____ (1937a). Analysis terminable and interminable. *Standard Edition* 23:209–270.

_____ (1937b). Constructions in analysis. *Standard Edition* 23:255–270.

_____ (1940). An outline of psychoanalysis. *Standard Edition* 23:141–208.

Friedman, L. (1992). How and why patients become more

objective. Sterba compared with Strachey. *Psychoanalytic Quarterly* 61:1–17.

Fromm, M. G. (1989). Winnicott's work in relationship to classical psychoanalysis and ego psychology. In *The Facilitating Environment*, ed. M.G. Fromm and B. C. Smith, pp. 3–26. Madison, CT: International Universities Press.

Gardner, M. R. (1983). *Self Inquiry*. Boston: Little, Brown.

Gaskill, H. S. (1980). The closing phase of the psychoanalytic treatment of adults and the goals of psychoanalysis: "the myth of perfectibility." *International Journal of Psycho-Analysis* 61:11–23.

Gill, M. M. (1954). Psychoanalysis and exploratory psychotherapy. *Journal of the American Psychoanalytic Association* 2:771–797.

––––– (1982). *Analysis of Transference*, vol. 1: *Theory and Technique*. New York: International Universities Press.

Glover, E. (1955). *The Technique of Psychoanalysis*. New York: International Universities Press.

Goldberger, M. (1989). Review of *Techniques of Working with Resistance*, ed. D. S. Milman and G. D. Goldman. *Psychoanalytic Quarterly* 58:295–298.

Gray, P. (1973). Psychoanalytic technique and the ego's capacity for viewing intrapsychic conflict. *Journal of the American Psychoanalytic Association* 21:474–494.

––––– (1982). "Developmental lag" in the evolution of technique for psychoanalysis of neurotic conflict. *Journal of the American Psychoanalytic Association* 30:621–655.

––––– (1986). On helping analysands observe intrapsychic activity. In *Psychoanalysis: The Science of Mental Conflict. Essays in Honor of Charles Brenner*, ed. A. D. Richards and M. S. Willick, pp. 245–268. Hillsdale, NJ: Analytic Press.

––––– (1987). On the technique of analysis of the superego—an introduction. *Psychoanalytic Quarterly* 56:130–154.

––––– (1990a). The nature of therapeutic action in psychoanalysis. *Journal of the American Psychoanalytic Association* 38:1083–1097.

_____ (1990b). A conversation with Paul Gray. *The American Psychoanalyst* 24:10–11

_____ (1991). On transferred permissiveness or approving superego functions: the analysis of the ego's superego activities. Part II. *Psychoanalytic Quarterly* 60:1–21.

_____ (1992). Memory as resistance and the telling of a dream. *Journal of the American Psychoanalytic Association* 40:307–326.

_____ (1994). *The Ego and Analysis of Defense*. Northvale, NJ: Jason Aronson.

Greenberg, J. (1991). *Oedipus and Beyond*. Cambridge, MA: Harvard University Press.

Greenberg, J., and Mitchell, S. A. (1983). *Object Relations and Psychoanalytic Theory*. Cambridge, MA: Harvard University Press.

Greenson, R. R. (1967). *The Technique and Practice of Psychoanalysis*. New York: International Universities Press.

Grinberg, L. (1968). On acting out and its role in the psychoanalytic process. *International Journal of Psycho-Analysis* 49:171–178.

Hartmann, H. (1939). *Ego Psychology and the Problem of Adaptation*. New York: International Universities Press, 1958.

_____ (1960). *Psychoanalysis and Moral Values*. New York: International Universities Press.

_____ (1964). *Essays on Ego Psychology*. New York: International Universities Press.

Hartmann, H., Kris, E., and Loewenstein, R. (1946). Comments on the function of psychic structure. *Psychoanalytic Study of the Child* 2:11–38. New York: International Universities Press.

_____ (1949). Notes on the theory of aggression. *Psychoanalytic Study of the Child* 3/4:9–36. New York: International Universities Press.

Herzog, P. (1991). *Conscious and Unconscious: Psychological Issues*. Monograph 58. New York: International Universities Press.

Inhelder, B., and Piaget, J. (1958). *The Growth of Logical Thinking from Childhood to Adolescence.* New York: Basic Books.

Jacobs, T. J. (1990). On beginning an analysis with a young adult. In *On Beginning an Analysis*, ed. T. Jacobs and A. Rothstein, pp. 83–100. Madison, CT: International Universities Press.

Jacobs, T. J., and Rothstein, A. (1990). *On Beginning an Analysis.* Madison, CT: International Universities Press.

Jacobson, J. G. (1992). Signal affects and our psychoanalytic confusion of tongues. Plenary address to the American Psychoanalytic Association, Washington, DC, May.

Joseph, B. (1988). Object relations in clinical practice. *Psychoanalytic Quarterly* 57:626–642.

Joseph, E. D. (1975). Clinical formulations and research. *Psychoanalytic Quarterly* 44:526–533.

_____ (1987). The consciousness of being conscious. *Journal of the American Psychoanalytic Association* 35:5–22.

Kafka, E. (1989). The contribution of Hartmann's adaptational theory to psychoanalysis, with special reference to regression and symptom formation. *Psychoanalytic Quarterly* 58:571–591.

Kantrowitz, J., Katz, A. L., and Paolitto, F. (1990). Followup of psychoanalysis five to ten years after termination: development of the self-analytic function. *Journal of the American Psychoanalytic Association* 38:605–636.

Kanzer, M. (1972). Superego aspects of free association and the fundamental rule. *Journal of the American Psychoanalytic Association* 20:246–266.

Katan, A. (1961). Some thoughts about the role of verbalization in early childhood. *Psychoanalytic Study of the Child* 16:184–188. New York: International Universities Press.

Kernberg, O. F. (1987). An ego psychological-object relations theory approach to the transference. *Psychoanalytic Quarterly* 56:197–221.

King, P., and Steiner, R. (1991). *The Freud–Klein Controversies 1941–45.* London: Routledge.

Klein, G. S. (1976). *Psychoanalytic Theory: An Exploration of Essentials*. New York: International Universities Press.

Kohut, H. (1984). *How Does Analysis Cure?* Chicago: University of Chicago Press.

Kohut, H., and Wolf, E. S. (1978). The disorders of the self and their treatment. *International Journal of Psycho-Analysis* 59:414–425.

Kris, A. O. (1982). *Free Association. Method and Process*. New Haven, CT: Yale University Press.

_____ (1983). The analyst's conceptual freedom in the method of free association. *International Journal of Psycho-Analysis* 64:407–411.

_____ (1990a). Helping patients by analyzing self criticism. *Journal of the American Psychoanalytic Association* 38:605–636.

_____ (1990b). The analyst's stance and the method of free association. *Psychoanalytic Study of the Child* 45:25–41. New Haven, CT: Yale University Press.

_____ (1992). Interpretation and the method of free association. *Psychoanalytic Inquiry* 12:208–224.

Kris, E. (1938). Review of "The Ego and Mechanisms of Defense." *International Journal of Psycho-Analysis* 19:347–348.

_____ (1951). Ego psychology and interpretation in psychoanalytic therapy. *Psychoanalytic Quarterly* 20:15–30.

_____ (1956a). On some vicissitudes of insight in psychoanalysis. *International Journal of Psycho-Analysis* 37: 445–455.

_____ (1956b). The personal myth. *Journal of the American Psychoanalytic Association* 4:653–681.

Kuhn, T. (1970). *The Structure of Scientific Revolutions* Chicago: University of Chicago Press.

Landau, B. (1995). The attribute of being in consciousness as a "beacon light" in a structural theory approach to developing specific psychoanalytic methods of technique: a perspective on the evolution of the concept. In *Undoing the Developmental Lag in Psychoanalytic Technique: Essays in Honor of Paul Gray*, ed. M. Goldberger, Northvale, NJ: Jason Aronson, in press.

Lear, J. (1990). *Love and Its Place in Nature*. New York: Farrar, Straus & Giroux.

Levy, S. T., and Inderbitzin, C. B. (1990). The analytic surface and the theory of technique. *Journal of the American Psychoanalytic Association* 38:371–392.

Lichtenberg, J. D., and Galler, F. (1987). The fundamental rule: a study of current usage. *Journal of the American Psychoanalytic Association* 35:47–76.

Loewald, H. (1960). Therapeutic action of psychoanalysis. *International Journal of Psycho-Analysis* 41:16–35.

_____ (1971). Some considerations on repetition and repetition compulsion. *International Journal of Psycho-Analysis* 52:59–66.

_____ (1975). Psychoanalysis as art and the fantasy character of the psychoanalytic situation. *Journal of the American Psychoanalytic Association* 23:277–299.

Loewenstein, R. M. (1963). Some considerations on free associations. *Journal of the American Psychoanalytic Association* 11:451–473.

_____ (1972). Ego autonomy and psychoanalytic technique. *Psychoanalytic Quarterly* 41:1–22.

Mahler, M. S., Pine, F., and Bergman, A. (1975). *The Psychological Birth of the Human Infant*. New York: Basic Books.

Mahoney, P. (1979). The boundaries of free association. *Psychoanalysis and Contemporary Thought* 2:151–198.

Malin, A. (1993). A self psychological approach to the analysis of resistances: a case report. *International Journal of Psycho-Analysis* 74:505–518.

McLaughlin, J. T. (1987). The play of transference: some reflections on enactment. *Journal of the American Psychoanalytic Association* 35:557–582.

_____ (1991). Clinical and theoretical aspects of enactment. *Journal of the American Psychoanalytic Association* 39:595–614.

Meyers, W. A. (1987). Actions speak louder than words. *Psychoanalytic Quarterly* 56:645–666.

Mitchell, S. A. (1988). *Relational Concepts in Psychoanalysis.* Cambridge, MA: Harvard University Press.

Modell, A. H. (1988). The centrality of the psychoanalytic setting and the changing aims of treatment: a perspective from a theory of object relations. *Psychoanalytic Quarterly* 57:577–596.

Moore, B. E., and Fine, B. D. (1990). *Psychoanalytic Terms and Concepts.* New Haven, CT: American Psychoanalytic Association and Yale University Press.

Mosher, P. M. (1991). *Title Key Word and Author Index to Psychoanalytic Journals, 1920–1990.* New York: American Psychoanalytic Association.

Myerson, P. G. (1960). Awareness and stress: post-psychoanalytic utilization of insight. *International Journal of Psycho-Analysis* 41:147–155.

——— (1981). The nature of transactions that enhance the progressive phase of a psychoanalysis. *International Journal of Psycho-Analysis* 62:91–105.

Nagel, E. (1961). *The Structure of Science.* New York: Harcourt, Brace, & World.

Novick, J. (1982). Termination: themes and issues. *Psychoanalytic Inquiry* 2:329–365.

Novick, J., and Novick, K. K. (1991). Some comments on masochism and the delusion of omnipotence from a development perspective. *Journal of the American Psychoanalytic Association* 39:307–332.

Nunberg, H. (1955). *Principles of Psychoanalysis.* New York: International Universities Press.

Panel. (1971). The basic rule: free association—a reconsideration. H. Seidman, rep. *Journal of the American Psychoanalytic Association* 19:98–109.

Paniagua, C. (1985). A methodological approach to surface material. *International Review of Psychoanalysis* 12:31–325.

——— (1991). Patient's surface, clinical surface, and workable surface. *Journal of the Amererican Psychoanalytic Association* 39:669–686.

Pfeffer, A. Z. (1961). Follow up study of a successful analysis. *Journal of the American Psychoanalytic Association* 9:698–718.

Piaget, J. (1926). *The Language and Thought of the Child.* New York: Harcourt, Brace.

—— (1930) *The Child's Conception of Physical Causality.* London: Kegan Paul.

Piaget, J., and Inhelder, B. (1959). *The Psychology of the Child.* New York: Basic Books.

Poland, W. S. (1992). From analytic surface to analytic space. *Journal of the American Psychoanalytic Association* 40:381–405.

Pray, M. (1994). Analyzing defenses: two different methods. *Journal of Clinical Psychoanalysis* 3:87–126.

Rapaport, D. (1967). *The Collected Papers of David Rapaport,* ed. M. M. Gill. New York: Basic Books.

Reich, W. (1933). *Character Analysis.* New York: Farrar, Straus, Cudahy, 1949.

Ritvo, S. (1978). The psychoanalytic process in childhood. *Psychoanalytic Study of the Child* 33:295–306. New Haven, CT: Yale University Press.

Roughton, R. (in press). Action and acting out. In *Psychoanalysis: The Major Concepts,* ed. B. E. Moore. New Haven, CT: Yale University Press.

Sandler, A.-M. (1975). Comments on the significance of Piaget's work for psychoanalysis. *International Review of Psycho-Analysis* 2:365–377.

Sandler, J., Kennedy, H., and Tyson, R. L. (1980). *The Technique of Child Analysis: Conversations with Anna Freud.* Cambridge, MA: Harvard University Press.

Schafer, R. (1970). An overview of Heinz Hartmann's contributions to psychoanalysis. *International Journal of Psycho-Analysis* 51:425–446.

—— (1983). *The Analytic Attitude.* New York: Basic Books.

Schlessinger, N., and Robbins, F. P. (1983). *A Developmental View of the Psychoanalytic Process: Follow-up Studies and Their Consequences*. New York: International Universities Press.

Scott, W. C. M. (1976). A neglected classic IV: M. Nina Searl's "The Psychology of Screaming." *Bulletin of the Philadelphia Association for Psychoanalysis* 3:117–119.

Searl, M. N. (1936). Some queries on principles of technique. *International Journal of Psycho-Analysis* 17:471–493.

_____ (1938). A note on the relation between physical and psychical differences in boys and girls. *International Journal of Psycho-Analysis* 19:50–62.

Shapiro, T., and Perry, R. (1976). Latency revisited. *Psychoanalytic Study of the Child* 31:79–105. New Haven, CT: Yale University Press.

Shaw, R. R. (1989). Hartmann on adaptation: an incomparable or incomprehensible legacy. *Psychoanalytic Quarterly* 58:592–611.

Smith, J. H. (1986). Dualism revisited: Schafer, Hartmann, and Freud. *Psychoanalytic Inquiry* 6:543–574.

Sonnenberg, S. M. (1991). The analyst's self analysis and its impact on clinical work: a comment on the sources and importance of personal insight. *Journal of the American Psychoanalytic Association* 39:687–704.

Spacal, S. (1990). Free association as a method of self observation in relation to other methodological principles of psychoanalysis. *Psychoanalytic Quarterly* 59:420–436.

Spitz, R. A. (1945). Hospitalism: an inquiry into the genesis of psychiatric conditions in early childhood. *Psychoanalytic Study of the Child* 1:53–74. New York: International Universities Press.

Steiner, J. (1994). Patient-centered and analyst-centered interpretations: some implications of containment and counter-transference. *Psychoanalytic Inquiry* 14:406–422.

Sterba, R. (1934). The fate of the ego in psychoanalytic therapy. *International Journal of Psycho-Analysis* 15:117–126.

_____ (1940). The dynamics of the dissolution of the transference resistance. *Psychoanalytic Quarterly* 9:363–375.

Stern, D. (1985). *The Interpersonal World of the Infant*. New York: Basic Books.

Stone, L. (1954). The widening scope of indications for psychoanalysis. *Journal of the American Psychoanalytic Association* 2:567–594.

_____ (1961). *The Psychoanalytic Situation*. New York: International Universities Press.

_____ (1973). On resistance to the psychoanalytic process: some thoughts on its nature and motivation. *Psychoanalysis and Contemporary Science* 2:42–73.

Strachey, J. (1959). Editor's introduction to inhibition, symptoms, and anxiety. *Standard Edition* 20:77–86.

Weinshel, E. M. (1984). Some observations on the psychoanalytic process. *Psychoanalytic Quarterly* 53:63–92.

_____ (1992). Therapeutic technique in psychoanalysis and psychoanalytic therapy. *Journal of the American Psychoanalytic Association* 40:327–348.

White, R. W. (1963). Ego and reality in psychoanalytic theory. *Psychological Issues*, Monograph 11. New York: International Universities Press.

Winnicott, D. W. (1965). *The Maturational Processes and the Facilitating Environment: Studies in the Theory of Emotional Development*. New York: International Universities Press.

_____ (1968). Interpretation in psychoanalysis. In *The Facilitating Environment*, ed. M. G. Fromm and B. C. Smith, pp. 629–636. Madison, CT: International Universities Press.

Wolff, P. H. (1967). Cognitive considerations for a psychoanalytic theory of language acquisition. In *Motives and Thought: Psychoanalytic Essays in Honor of David Rapaport*, ed. R. R. Holt. Psychological Issues 5, Monograph 18/19:299–342.

Wyman, H. M. (1989). Hartmann, health, and homosexuality: some clinical aspects of "Ego Psychology and the Problem of Adaptation." *Psychoanalytic Quarterly* 58:612–639.

CREDITS

The author gratefully acknowledges permission to reprint the following:

Chapter 2: Originally titled "In the Neighborhood: Aspects of a Good Interpretation and a 'Developmental Lag' in Ego Psychology," by Fred Busch, in *Journal of the American Psychoanalytic Association*, vol. 41, #1, pp. 151–177. Reprinted with modifications. Copyright © 1993 by International Universities Press.

Chapter 3: Originally titled "Some Ambiguities in the Method of Free Association and Their Implications for Technique," by Fred Busch, in *Journal of the American Psychoanalytic Association*, vol. 42, #2, pp. 363–374. Reprinted with modifications. Copyright © 1994 by International Universities Press.

Chapter 4: Originally titled "Beginning a Psychoanalytic Treatment: Establishing an Analytic Frame," by Fred Busch, in *Journal of the American Psychoanalytic As-*

sociation, accepted for publication. Copyright © 1995 by International Universities Press.

Chapter 5: Originally titled "Recurring Thoughts on Unconscious Ego Resistances," by Fred Busch, in *Journal of the American Psychoanalytic Association,* vol. 40, #4, pp. 1089–1115. Reprinted with modifications. Copyright © 1992 by International Universities Press.

Chapter 6: Originally titled "Do Actions Speak Louder Than Words? A Query into an Enigma in Analytic Theory and Technique," by Fred Busch, in *Journal of the American Analytic Association,* vol. 43, #1. Copyright © 1995 by International Universities Press.

Chapter 8: Originally titled "An Unknown Classic: M. N. Searl's (1936) 'Some Queries on Principles of Technique,'" by Fred Busch, in *The Psychoanalytic Quarterly,* accepted for publication. Copyright © 1995 by *The Psychoanalytic Quarterly.*

Chapter 9: Originally titled "Resistance Analysis and Object Relations Theory: Erroneous Conceptions amidst Some Timely Contributions," by Fred Busch, in *Psychoanalytic Psychology,* vol. 12, pp. 43—53. Copyright © 1995 Lawrence Erlbaum Associates, Inc.

Excerpts from "Some Queries on Principles of Technique," by M. N. Searl, in *International Journal of Psycho-Analysis,* 1936, vol. 17, pp. 471–493. Copyright © 1936 by the Institute of Psycho-Analysis.

INDEX